Ownership
Thinking

Ownership Thinking

How to End Entitlement
and Create a Culture
of Accountability,
Purpose, and Profit

BRAD HAMS

New York Chicago San Francisco Lisbon London Madrid Mexico City
Milan New Delhi San Juan Seoul Singapore Sydney Toronto

The *McGraw·Hill* Companies

Copyright © 2012 by Brad Hams. All rights reserved. Printed in the United States of America. Except as permitted under the United States Copyright Act of 1976, no part of this publication may be reproduced or distributed in any form or by any means, or stored in a database or retrieval system, without the prior written permission of the publisher.

5 6 7 8 9 10 DOC/DOC 1 6 5 4 3 2

ISBN 978-0-07-177245-7
MHID 0-07-177245-6

e-ISBN 978-0-07-177346-1
e-MHID 0-07-177346-0

McGraw-Hill books are available at special quantity discounts to use as premiums and sales promotions or for use in corporate training programs. To contact a representative, please e-mail us at bulksales@mcgraw-hill.com.

This book is printed on acid-free paper.

Dedicated to the memory of Ayn Rand

CONTENTS

■ CHAPTER FIVE

Get RIP'd: Rapid Improvement Plans 151

■ CHAPTER SIX

Employee Stock Ownership Plans (ESOPs): Do Ownership Thinkers Have to Own? 181

■ CHAPTER SEVEN

Ownership Thinking for the
Long Term 195

ACKNOWLEDGMENTS

Thanks to my mom and dad for delivering me into this incredible world of opportunity.

Thanks to my wife, Carmen, for cheering me on over the years and for her help in creating and growing our concept and company.

Thanks to Alex Freytag, my excellent partner and vice president at Ownership Thinking, for his feedback and ideas.

Thanks to Judith Bardwick for starting me on the publishing journey and for her invaluable help with ideas and content in the book.

Thanks to my literary consultant, Laurie Harper, for her encouragement and her help in writing my book proposal.

Thanks to Cynthia Zigmund, my agent, for her fantastic support and help in finding a publisher.

This Is Not
Your Typical
Business Book

In 1973, at 17 years of age, I left my home in Scottsdale, Arizona, and hitchhiked to Berkeley. I was the youngest of three kids, and my brother and sister had both gone to Pomona College in California—a rather expensive private school. We were comfortable enough when I was a child, and though my dad didn't make a huge amount of money as a structural engineer and my mom didn't work at the time, we lived in middle-class neighborhoods and went to decent public schools. Although I've never talked much about it with my dad, I assume that putting my brother and sister through college (even though they contributed) was not an easy task for him. I'd gotten into a bit of trouble a year or so before I left home, and to be honest, I wasn't the best student in high school (although I did graduate). I should qualify that statement. I was, in fact, a good student, but perhaps a different kind of student. I read incessantly, but I just was not particularly engaged in school. Given this, it is understandable that my dad was not all that interested in paying for me to go to college, no doubt thinking it a dubious investment at best. So he told me that he didn't think that college was all that important and did not intend to help me out with it.

So, I hitchhiked to Berkeley. I was angry about the situation at home, and I suppose in the back of my mind I was thinking something along these lines: "I'll show everyone. I don't need help from anyone, and I can take care of myself anyway." I'd gotten hooked on skiing while in Arizona (yes, there is skiing in Arizona), and I thought working at a ski shop would be cool. I pounded the pavement going to every ski and sporting goods shop in the area until one hired me. I worked full time at Kelly's Sporting Goods for a few years, making something like $2.50 an hour at first, and I skied every chance I had. And I read incessantly.

I left Kelly's at some point and began working at a boot store in Oakland. I worked my way up to store manager and ran their location in Walnut Creek. I was there for a few years (taking a six-month hiatus at one point to travel through Europe), then went on to take a manager position with a bakery / café chain in the San Francisco area, which looked like a good opportunity since it had recently been purchased by PepsiCo. I worked at PepsiCo for several years, working my way up in operations and finance and eventually into leadership roles in their corporate office. During that time, I also put myself through college, obtaining an undergraduate and a graduate degree at the University of San Francisco. Ultimately, I went on to run a business in Mexico and founded a successful consulting company in 1995.

I believe that life is largely about learning and growth. My opinion that neither of these is exclusively found in the classroom probably doesn't surprise you, after reading the short biography above. School has been important to my learning and growth; however, I have learned far more by surrounding myself with intelligent people, by experiencing life, by taking risks, and by struggling and even failing on occasion. My learning has also come from reading. From a young age, reading has been a significant part of my life. I read anything and everything: business books, political books, self-help books, motivational books, textbooks, spiritual books, psychology books, and an occasional novel. Also, I stay on top of current events by reading several newspapers and various Internet publications and blogs.

I am telling you about my life for several reasons. I want to point out that I am something of a self-made man and that I believe lifelong learning and personal achievement are among the most important things in life. I mentioned earlier that I was angry when I left home. My perspective at that time didn't leave room for understanding why I was not going to have the same opportunities *given to me* that were given to my brother and sister. Today, I am immensely grateful for how my adult life started and progressed. Were I not in a position of great need and significant personal motivation, it is unlikely that I would have achieved the things I've achieved, learned the things I've learned, and had the opportunity to help the people and businesses I've helped. This great country that I was blessed to be born in has grown more self-made, brilliant, and inspirational people than any other country on earth. Why? Because the United States of America was founded by and has prospered as a result of people who escaped oppression and desired to create a life of liberty stemming from solid values and hard work. And by God, they did.

As we Americans have prospered over the decades, I'm afraid we have lost sight of what made us great. We have become a bit soft and have created more and more entitlements that allow us to have smaller lives focused on day-to-day satisfactions and gratifications that are, in the great scheme of life, not all that compelling. I am saddened by this and, on occasion, greatly disturbed by the direction I see us heading.

This book is not your typical business book for more than one reason. In it, I am going to introduce you to a way of doing business that will demand quite a bit from you and from all of your employees. It is a way of doing business that requires literally everyone in an organization to participate in the business of the business, not just the tasks they happen to perform in it. It requires that people take responsibility for becoming better and more knowledgeable every day. It requires that they are active participants in their organization's financial success and ultimately their own. I also hope to convince you that, although your employees may not know it, this is what most of them, deep in their hearts and souls, really want. I know from experience that it will make them happier and more fulfilled.

This is not your typical business book also because over the years I've learned that business is not only about business. There is an important spiritual side of great companies. There is also a political element to business that needs to be confronted, as well as a psychological component. And, of course, there is the human and emotional side of businesses. I am fully aware that this thinking can be somewhat controversial. Maybe it would be ideal to write a book that creates no basis for contention or argument and that is accepted with enthusiasm by every reader. Of course, that would be unrealistic, and an effort to do it would most likely result in a wishy-washy tome with significantly less value than what I hope this book will provide. Therefore, I will do my best to present my experience and observations in a manner that will engage and not offend. I have implemented Ownership Thinking in virtually every type of industry at this point (profit and non-profit) and with people of many different political leanings, religious beliefs, and ethnic backgrounds. *All* of them have benefited from pursuing this way of doing business, and I would venture to say that they have benefited both professionally and personally.

The Origin of Ownership Thinking

Prior to 1990, most of my career had been in operations and finance. I held leadership positions at PepsiCo for several years and also at Mrs. Fields Cookies. My education was quite far removed from finance, however. I had gone to college in my twenties for a couple of years, but wasn't very clear on what I wanted from it, so I went back to work (I have had jobs since the age of 12). I decided in my thirties that change management was interesting, so I enrolled at the University of San Francisco (USF) and got an undergraduate degree in organizational behavior and a graduate degree in organizational development and human resources (finishing at the rather late age of 35). I am grateful for this unusual mix of operations, finance, and human resources because it has led me to look at business quite holistically. I understand that when you sum it all up, business is about making money, so I have made it a point to become very literate in the area of finance. However, I also look at business from the human resource perspective, knowing that you can be financially focused, but can do so in an interactive, high-involvement, transparent, and far more enjoyable way than what the vast majority of companies out there are currently doing.

After finishing my graduate degree, I began to tire of working in a corporate environment where personal agendas were prevalent and decision making was sluggish, so I started a one-man consulting company in 1990 called Action Research. I borrowed the name from a methodology I learned while going to school at USF. The name of my company has changed twice since that time, and I'm quite certain that the name we've had for the last 15 years now will be our last: Ownership Thinking. I love the name of our company because it communicates perfectly what we want to achieve: the creation of organizations whose employees think and act like owners toward creating wealth (which, in turn, creates opportunity). Ownership Thinking goes beyond this, however, and is also about creating great cultures that are fun and rewarding to work in.

To be honest, I was rather clueless when I first went into business about what it meant to be a consultant (I've since learned that there are more than a few clueless consultants running around). Given this, I was simply looking for any project that I thought might fit my rather unusual background. As luck would have it, Mrs. Fields was looking for someone to help it with its international development. The company representative called me shortly after I'd hung out my consulting shingle, and I agreed to give the company 50 percent of my time for a while to help (no one had to twist my arm much). If you are unfamiliar with Mrs. Fields Cookies, it is primarily a retail cookie and baked-goods chain. At the time, it had in operation several hundred locations domestically and did over $200 million in annual revenue. After spending a couple of years opening up cookie companies around the world, I began supporting the licensee for Mexico, a company by the name of Bimbo, with their development of the Mrs. Fields brand. Bimbo (pronounced "Beembo" in Spanish) is a multi-billion dollar bread products manufacturer and distributor based in Mexico City and now a big player in the United States, as well.

In 1992, after about six months in business, the Mexico operation (MFD de México) had eight locations open and a small corporate office and was nowhere near to meeting its financial plan. Ownership was very concerned about this, and during one of my visits, they asked me if I'd be interested in moving to Mexico City to take the reins as president of MFD. I decided that moving to Mexico might be a once-in-a-lifetime opportunity, so I took the job.

I knew that MFD de México was having some difficulties, but I had a good deal of experience with the Mrs. Fields concept, and felt confident that the company could be turned around with the right leadership. It was a bit frightening when I arrived, however, to discover that none of the employees seemed very concerned that the company wasn't performing well. Not wanting to waste any time (or having the luxury to do so), I dug into why this might be the case and discovered a few things very quickly about doing business in Mexico. First, management is very centralized, and in most organizations, virtually all decisions are made at the very top. In addition, very little information is shared with employees—especially financial information. So, my assumption regarding employees' lack of concern was not accurate: they just didn't know that the company wasn't performing well. The second issue in Mexico is the huge disparity in wages. Senior-level people make pretty good money—more or less what we are accustomed to in the United States—and everyone else makes next to nothing. When I arrived to take over my responsibilities, employees working in the Mrs. Fields Mexico retail locations were making substantially less money per hour than it cost to buy one cookie in their stores.

Paradoxically, I also learned that the people in Mexico (by and large) are extraordinarily entrepreneurial. I have noticed this in developing countries in general, and I believe it is due to the levels of poverty. In Mexico, 2 percent of the population is wealthy (and I mean *really* wealthy), 8 percent is middle class, and 90 percent is poor (by our standards). Given this, being entrepreneurial (constantly looking for opportunities) is just a survival mechanism. Add to this the extreme volatility of the economics, and people grow up understanding that if an opportunity presents itself, they'd better take it now because it may not be there tomorrow. I learned about this volatility firsthand. Near the end of my second year as president of MFD, the peso lost half of its value overnight—literally. At the time, we were importing all of our product; a frozen dough product manufactured in Southern California. Our cost of goods doubled. In addition, the government raised interest rates to an astonishing 107 percent after the devaluation to encourage investors to keep their money in the country, even if they were simply banking it to take advantage of these high rates. Unfortunately, MFD was holding several hundred thousand dollars in debt at the time, so our interest payments became crippling. Incredibly, we survived this (many companies did not), and I'm convinced that we did because we had created a culture and a way of doing business that was extraordinarily powerful on many different levels. It was simple. It got results. It was fun. It developed people. And, it got to the heart of what drives me, both personally and from a business perspective—the notion of eradicating entitlement (more on this in Chapter 1).

To reiterate, when I arrived in Mexico none of the MFD employees knew that the company was struggling. They were making very little money. But they were very entrepreneurial, and I sensed that they would like to get more involved in the business and would certainly like to make more money. How could we capitalize on this? After pondering it for a few weeks, my staff and I came up with a program that we called Socios. *Socios* is a

Spanish word, which translates roughly to "partners" in English. This fit beautifully with the message we wanted to convey: We're all partners in this effort to turn things around here.

Fundamentally, there were three components to Socios, which later became the principal elements of Ownership Thinking (the name of our process is the same as the name of our company). If you consider the desired result—which is to create an organization of employees who think and act like owners—then these elements are quite logical (perhaps even intuitive).

First, if a business is financially successful, the owner is financially successful. So, we figured we needed a method of rewarding employees if they were successful in turning the financial performance of the company around. My experience with incentive plans had not been very positive in the past, so I knew we had to be careful here. Most incentive plans are not only ineffective, but also actually damaging to the company. Why? They are far too complicated. They are typically tied to financial performance, but employees are not taught anything about finance, much less the specifics of how they are supposed to fund their plan. In fact, they are not even taught that incentive plans must be self-funding. Therefore, in a typical incentive plan, there is little connection between what employees actually do and the incentive dollars they receive or don't receive. So what happens? They get to the end of a quarter (given that the plan provides for a quarterly payout) and receive a big bonus check. They don't know why, but, of course, they are happy to receive this "gift." Perhaps they receive bonuses for several consecutive quarters.

Let's stop for a moment and consider something: What is the purpose of an incentive plan? I believe that its purpose is to shape employees' behavior toward improving the financial performance of the company. The typical plan, described in the previous paragraph, is clearly not doing this; it is simply an entitlement. And, as I alluded to earlier, this plan will ultimately damage the company. Why? Because eventually there will be a quarter with poor business performance. Employees don't know this because they have not been seeing financial information and have not been engaged. The only thing they know is that they will not be getting a bonus this quarter. What do you suppose they are thinking now? Given how they have been conditioned, they are most likely thinking that they are getting screwed. The thinking goes something like this: "I'm doing the same thing I always did. I always got this money before. *They* must be doing something." Now we have a morale problem. This is very frustrating for business owners. They created an incentive plan to change behavior and improve performance (and to give something back), but the outcome is (1) little or no change in behavior, (2) a new expense, and (3) an angry and ungrateful workforce.

Given these considerations, I knew I had to be cautious about any reward system that I designed and provided for employees at MFD. The design of the plan had to be simple and understandable, and it had to be directly tied to the improved financial performance of the company. What we learned at MFD (and from considerable research I've done since my work with MFD) is discussed in detail in Chapter 2.

My staff and I also thought we'd better teach the employees about the business and how it made money—the next component of Ownership Thinking. If one wants an organization of employees who think and act like owners, then those employees had better have some understanding of how companies operate and make money and how their jobs affect the company's operational and financial performance. To accomplish this, we developed a program to teach everyone at MFD the basics of business and finance, helping them to understand how that all worked and how the tasks they performed affected the business from a financial perspective. I will discuss how to educate employees in finance and why I believe it is important in Chapter 3.

Finally, we created a way for everyone to get involved in monitoring and measuring the company's performance so that we could follow our progress in a highly visible fashion. While considering how we might do this, we looked at how companies typically monitor performance, or keep score, which is with their financial statements. We then asked ourselves a few questions:

- Is this method of keeping score engaging everyone?

- Do employees typically see financial statements? Would they understand them if they did see them?

- Do financial statements focus on the things that create financial performance or simply on the financial result itself?

- Given the above, is this method of keeping score proactive or reactive?

- Do financial statements help to create an environment of visibility and accountability?

The answers to these questions were obvious. We then considered what we might do differently and decided that the best approach might be to create an environment something akin to a game. Most people enjoy games and become engaged when they play them, no doubt because people like to have fun and because (almost universally) they like to win. So, we created a scoreboard. But instead of things like runs, hits, and errors, we focused on those leading, measurable *activities* that drove our financial performance (we now call these Key Performance Indicators, or KPIs) and got everyone focused on those. More about this in Chapter 4.

These became the three components of Socios, now called Ownership Thinking: The Right Incentives, The Right Education, and The Right Measures (we have since added The Right People, which is the foundation of any good company and one of the outcomes of practicing Ownership Thinking). We designed and rolled out the program a few months after my arrival in Mexico, and the results were even better than I had hoped for. We had a significant operational and financial turnaround in very short order (in fact, we doubled our profitability in less than a year). Just as important, however, was the effect this had on the employees: they became engaged, they had fun, they made more money, and several of them became leaders.

Upon returning to the United States and settling in Denver, I fleshed out the details of a model based on our experience at MFD and created something I was confident could be replicated in virtually any industry (a belief that has proved to be true). As of this book's publication, Ownership Thinking LLC has helped over 1,000 companies to implement Ownership Thinking throughout the United States, Canada, and Australia. The results have been truly inspirational.

In addition to the chapters detailed above, Chapters 5 and 6 will provide you with other tools available to lead your organization toward Ownership Thinking, including Rapid Improvement Plans (Chapter 5) and Employee Stock Ownership Plans (Chapter 6). In Chapter 7, you will find the tools we have created at Ownership Thinking that will help you tap into the community of business leaders and organizations that have created cultures of employees who think and act like owners toward creating wealth, opportunity, accountability, and purpose. Using the tools and information detailed in this book is your first step toward joining this community.

CHAPTER ONE

Why Ownership Thinking Is Desperately Needed

I love the name of our company (also the name we have coined for this way of doing business). The name *Ownership Thinking* describes exactly what we are trying to achieve. That is to say, to create cultures of employees who think and act like owners, *with the purpose of creating wealth*. I am a big fan of wealth, because wealth creates opportunities. With the information you will glean from this book, you will be able to create new wealth in your organization. Every employee in your organization will participate in creating wealth, and every employee in the organization will benefit from it.

It is important to point out that wealth creation is not a zero-sum game. We are often led to believe that if wealth is created somewhere, it must somehow be taking wealth away from somewhere (and, therefore, someone) else. Nothing could be further from the truth. The creation of wealth allows for investment of that wealth to create more wealth. And when employees are taught to engage in wealth creation, they become better stewards of wealth and are equipped to create wealth in their own right. One of my favorite examples of this is the Springfield ReManufacturing Corporation (SRC); I had a great deal of exposure to this company from 1995 to 2003 or so, and I owe a debt of gratitude for what I learned from that experience. SRC, which rebuilds big-vehicle engines, was established in 1983 when 13 employees purchased it from the failing International Harvester with $100,000 of their own money and (remarkably) $8.9 million in loans. At that time, the company did roughly $17 million in revenue and employed 120 people. By 1988, SRC's debt to equity ratio was down to 1.8 to 1, and the business had a value of $43 million. Since 1983, SRC (an employee-owned and open-book company) has founded and invested in more than 35 separate companies that do everything from consulting to packaging to building high-performance engines. Many of these companies are the brainchilds of SRC's employees, who have gone on to develop them under the SRC umbrella. The company now has sales of over $400 million per year and employs over 1,200 people.

Ownership Thinking is not only about wealth creation, however. It is also about creating extraordinary organizational cultures—cultures where employees learn the business of the business and are active participants; where everyone is challenged and must take responsibility for their company's destiny and their role within it; where workers know what the heck is going on and how they contribute; where everyone is a "part of"; and where people have fun.

How Owners and Employees Think

In order for companies to create wealth and extraordinary organizational cultures, employees and owners must become more aligned in their thinking. When I ask business owners what concerns they have, what they think about from day to day, or what might keep them awake at night, they generally mention the following:

- **Profit.** The company must have more revenue than it does expenses.

- **Cash flow.** Business owners understand that it's pretty difficult to run a business without cash. They also understand that a company can be profitable on paper, but run out of cash (more on this later).

- **Risk.** They have to face the realities of market conditions, the economy, liability, employee issues, and on and on. Business owners often have their personal wealth at stake as well, and their families will be impacted if the company is not successful.

- **Competition.** They must be able to compete in the marketplace in terms of quality, price, availability, and so on.

- **Employees.** They are faced with hiring and retaining the right employees, employee interaction, legal issues around employment, and so on.

- **Cost controls.** They must be able to keep costs in line to ensure that the company is profitable and generates cash. And there are many costs: materials, labor, regulatory, facilities, utilities, transportation, administrative, equipment maintenance, outside services, research and development, and marketing to name just a few. Oh, and don't forget taxes.

So that is what I hear from business owners. However, when I ask employees what concerns they have, what they think about from day to day, the list is quite different. I typically hear the following:

- My paycheck

- Benefits and health care

- Getting my work done

- Job security

- Recognition

- Friday (time off)

- The work environment (Do I like it here?)

- Opportunities for growth and/or more money

I am not being critical here; I'm simply telling you what I hear. Now, ask yourself what the list immediately above (the employee list) is all about. It is, of course, all about "me." The list from business owners, on the other hand, is about the business. It's about the business's financial performance, ability to compete, and overall sustainability. Fundamentally, Ownership Thinking is about moving employees away from *only* the "me" way of thinking and toward the concerns of the business and its financial performance. I say "only" because, of course, the list of personal concerns that employees have will not disappear by doing this. The paycheck, benefits, recognition, time off, and so on, will always be important to them. The point is, when employees are given the tools, information, and training to become more engaged in the business, the business will become more profitable—guaranteed. With more financial resources available to it, the business is able to take better care of its employees. It can do this with self-funded incentive plans (described later), potentially better benefit opportunities (or not taking them away, as many companies have done), and certainly better growth opportunities within the company because the company is more successful. Ownership Thinking is a win–win way of doing business.

In this book, I will be providing you with the tools and information you will need to pursue an Ownership Thinking culture in your organization. As I mentioned earlier, however, there are several important and profound reasons for practicing Ownership Thinking that go beyond operations and finance. And so, before we get into the tools, I will be addressing some of those reasons.

Entitlement

My mission in life is to eradicate entitlement, and Ownership Thinking is the tool I've created to help accomplish that mission. People with an entitlement mentality believe they are somehow owed something, that they should get things simply because they exist. Judith Bardwick, my friend and the author of nine terrific books, introduces the concept of entitlement in her important book *Danger in the Comfort Zone*:

> Entitlement is an attitude, a way of looking at life. Those who have this attitude believe that they do not have to earn what they get. They get what they want because of *who*

they are, not because of *what they do*. When this rich nation stopped requiring performance as a condition for keeping a job or getting a raise, it created a widespread attitude of Entitlement. Entitlement destroys motivation. It lowers productivity. In the long run it crushes self-esteem.

Entitlement has become an enormous problem in our culture, and I'm afraid it's getting worse with every generation. Ironically, I believe this has happened in large part because of our fanatical insistence that self-esteem, particularly in children, trumps virtually everything else. In fact, if we do not validate our kids' self-esteem, we may be considered hateful or mean or simply a bad parent. Under the pressure of this politically correct notion, we have been led to believe that it is our responsibility as parents to *give* self-esteem to our children. How have we done this? Have we done it by instilling discipline and the importance of a strong work ethic? On the contrary, we've lowered the standards in our schools so that everyone gets good grades. We don't keep score in games so that "everyone is a winner" (I recently attended a grade school award ceremony where there was a fifteenth-place ribbon with 15 participants in the event). We continually tell our children that they are performing wonderfully, even if they aren't. We've given them more and more, and required less and less of them.

The underlying theme of what I just described is that failure is not acceptable—even when a person is failing. Given this, we attempt to deal with failure in one of two ways. First, we deny that it is actually failure. We do this by lowering standards or by simply saying that success is not all that important; merely trying is enough (unfortunately, denying reality does not make it go away). Second, we continually rescue our kids. Rather than rescuing them by ensuring that they have the discipline to improve, we rescue them by attempting to fix the symptoms (poor grades, not enough stuff, lack of recognition, etc.). We have lost sight of the fact that sometimes people and organizations need to fail in order to become successful. In the 30 years before his election to the presidency of the United States, Abraham Lincoln suffered a myriad of failures and setbacks. Defeat is part of life, and, in fact, it often inspires—if we are taught to dust ourselves off and move on. Of course we will never learn to do this if we are constantly being rescued. Nor will we grow. It could be argued that Lincoln's failures eventually led him to greatness.

By the way, I suggest you reread the previous paragraph on entitlement, replacing the word *parent* with *employer*, and the word *children* (or *kids*) with *employees*. I think the same scenarios often apply in the workplace.

Here's an example of protecting our children from the reality of varying levels of talent or success that really floored me. I was in Seattle with a client some time ago and read a news item about a local elementary school that had banned students' use of Lego toys. The students had been building model houses and other buildings with the Legos, and since some constructions were larger and more impressive than others, the administration contended that the use of Legos might be damaging to the self-esteem of the students who were not particularly creative or ambitious. Further, and even more frightening, the administration maintained that Legos were promoting capitalism (heaven forbid!) and private ownership. They were banned in an effort to protect self-esteem and to "reeducate" students on the importance of collectivism.

All of these actions are taken with the goal of creating self-esteem. But wait a minute. What actually creates self-esteem? Is it having things? Is it being told we are doing well when in fact we are not? Is it bringing everyone down to the same common denominator? Or is it accomplishment? When we look solidly at this issue, self-esteem is only created through accomplishment. It cannot be given. It must be earned. As Ayn Rand states in *Capitalism, The Unknown Ideal*, "It would never occur to a person of self-esteem and independent judgment that one's 'identity' is a thing to be gained from or determined by others."

The insidious truth is that what is being done to create self-esteem in children is actually destroying it or perhaps preventing it from being developed at all. We are, in fact, *creating entitlement mentalities.* As Charles Sykes states in *50 Rules Kids Won't Learn in School,* "The reality that the self-esteem movement ignores is that children learn to feel good about themselves by actually acquiring skills: this is called self-confidence. Ask yourself if it is better to *feel good* about your swimming abilities, or to actually *know how to swim*."

The development of entitlement in children has carried over into adulthood and the world of education, work, and real life. Many people now expect to be taken care of and, in fact, have been taught that they will be. What follows are several "rights" that have been extolled by various politicians and platforms over the past several decades:

- The right to a useful and remunerative job

- The right to earn enough to provide adequate food, clothing, and recreation

- The right of every family to a decent home

- The right to adequate medical care

- The right to adequate protection from the economic fears of old age, sickness, accidents, and unemployment

- The right to a good education

I am not a cold-blooded person; in fact, quite the contrary is true. And I'm not opposed to altruism when it is appropriate. However, I believe that the notion of providing the things noted above to all citizens begs the following questions: At whose expense are these rights to be provided? From whose effort? And at the risk of sounding insensitive—why? In *Danger*, Judith Bardwick states: "Expressed simply, entitlement is the result of too much generosity. We give people what they expect and we don't hold them accountable for meeting criteria of excellence. In business it commonly happens because *managers are unwilling to do the work of requiring work*." Perhaps these managers have simply given up in the face of rampant entitlement and political correctness. Bardwick goes on to say: "When people don't have to earn what they get, they soon take for granted what they receive. The real irony is that they're not grateful for what they get. Instead, they want more. Too much security is what entitlement is all about."

In his important (and disturbing) book, *Weapons of Mass Instruction*, John Taylor Gatto delves into this issue as he analyzes the problems created by compulsory education. "Maturity," he says, "has by now been banished from nearly every aspect of our lives. Easy divorce laws have removed the need to work at relationships; easy credit has removed the need for fiscal self-control; easy entertainment has removed the need for people to learn to entertain themselves; easy answers have removed the need to ask questions. We have become a nation of children, happy to surrender our judgments and our wills to political exhortations and commercial blandishments that would insult actual adults."

At the heart of entitlement is the notion that if I want something I should be able to have it. Obviously everyone cannot have things simply because they want them. Someone must produce those things, and despite what we might hear, production is a private choice, not a public duty. From my experience, the people who actually produce things do so primarily for two reasons: (1) They have a strong work ethic. In other words, they have come to believe that rewards come only with hard work, and (2) They *enjoy* producing. It is exciting for them, and the reward for producing is not only the things they are able to afford as a result of it, but the personal growth and sense of worth that come from producing: that is, *true* self-esteem. Who, then, gets things simply because they feel entitled to them? They are typically the nonproducers.

I believe this is the direction we are headed in the United States of America: from each according to his ability, to each according to his need. Or perhaps it is more accurate to say: from each according to his work ethic, to each according to his want. I also know that, aside from the moral implications of this trend, this is a direction that must ultimately fail. There are many reasons for my thinking, but one of the fundamental contributors is simply this: if producers in the United States are punished for producing,

11

why should they continue to produce (in the United States, at any rate)? And if there are no producers, how will the nonproducers get the things they feel they are entitled to? Consider this statement by Francisco d'Anconia from Ayn Rand's *Atlas Shrugged*:

> You wish to see the fruits of my efforts taken by people who drift from failure to failure and expect me to pay their bills, who hold their wishing as an equivalent to my work and their need as a higher claim to reward than my effort, who proclaim that I am born to serfdom by reason of my genius while they are born to rule by the grace of their incompetence, that mine is to produce but theirs is to consume.

In addition to preventing the development of true self-esteem, entitlement in the workplace also lowers productivity. In organizations where entitlement is prevalent, employees are not held accountable for achieving results; therefore results (logically) are not achieved. In fact, results may not even be defined. I find that in these organizations, "busyness" is held in very high regard, and rewards are often tied to activity rather than performance. The following is an *unedited* e-mail I received from an employee in one of my client organizations, which illustrates my point:

> You recently spoke to the outfit I work for. you effectively lowered morale with your don't deserve a raise spiel. what abot exploitive employers who withhold raises from employees that deserve it because they earned it? you're doing a lot of harm to people who have worked very hard.

This e-mail came from an underperforming employee in a company that had been barely breaking even for the previous five years. What follows is a portion of my reply:

> Thank you for taking the time to write to me. I believe I remember you. When I was discussing incentive plans, you made a comment that you believed employees should receive both incentive rewards and salary increases. Perhaps you didn't hear my answer, or perhaps you chose not to hear it because you had already made your mind up about me. In nearly all cases, the companies that practice the Ownership Thinking methodology of doing business provide both salary increases (as they have historically done in most cases) and incentive opportunities (which are often far greater). Notice that I said *opportunities*. In other words, incentives (and salary increases, in my opinion) must be earned. One of the indisputable truths in business is that, in order for either to take place, the company must make a profit. I respect your comment about hard work; however, activity and results are not the same. When I work with clients, it is my goal to help employees in those companies to better understand the business and to receive the education and tools they need to become active participants in improving the profitability of the organization. In this way, the organization has more financial resources that it can (and should) share with its employees.

The Good News

We are not doomed to follow the path of entitlement, however. Why? Because in my experience working with thousands of employees and leaders in hundreds of companies over the past two decades, I have found that the vast majority of these people want to engage and want to contribute, and feel much better about themselves when they have the opportunity to do so. I have also found that, despite what many people believe, most of them have the capacity to do so.

The entitlement mentality I have described is in effect creating a culture that is very "me centric." In my work and life, I have observed that the further people go down this path, the more miserable they become. Why? Because "me" is actually quite small and limited. The further people get into self, the less involvement they have in anything outside of self, and therefore they lack purpose. Not only do these people lack purpose, in their hearts they cannot hide from the fact that they have not earned what they have. In addition, they may now be living in fear—fear of losing what they are now dependent on and lack the confidence to achieve on their own. People need a sense of accomplishment and a sense of purpose in order to be truly happy. So what exactly is this "purpose"? In a business environment, it may simply be the creation of a wonderful culture—an environment that is challenging, exciting, and rewarding (financially and otherwise). And once an organization reaches one level of enlightenment, it will likely search out other avenues of expression, such as community involvement or other forms of getting out of self (just as individuals do). The British philosopher John Stuart Mill noted that the only people who are truly happy are those "who have their minds fixed on some object other than their own happiness."

Abraham Maslow, the man who gave us Maslow's Hierarchy of Needs, once said: "The only happy people I know are the ones who are working well at something they consider important." I have also found that purposeful organizations are more profitable, and purposeful individuals are more financially secure. This is true in part because they have escaped the feelings of scarcity and fear that tend to accompany entitlement and have entered a world of abundance and serenity. They believe in themselves and their abilities. Though people may be drawn to security, I believe they are actually happier in liberty.

Judith Bardwick states that the opposite of entitlement is an attitude or mentality of earning, which she calls the "natural high of success." The following is from *Danger*:

> The climate of Earning is purposeful, disciplined energy.
> An Earning environment requires realistic opportunities
> to achieve and realistic requirements to do so. It requires
> parameters of achievement so there's pressure to perform
> and some certainty when you have performed. It requires
> accurate matching of requirements to ability so that you're
> right more often than you're wrong. People with a psychol-
> ogy of Earning know they're winners, but they also know
> they're always being judged. And they are not afraid. To
> people with a mind-set of Earning, that medium level of
> pressure makes things exciting. People discover that when
> they accept risk, they benefit. The attitude of Earning

recognizes this basic fact of human psychology: People prefer accountability; they want to be rewarded when they work hard and they want those who don't to be punished. For them, trying is not enough; accomplishment will be a requirement for respect.

People are tougher than we may think they are. More often than not, people will rise to the occasion when given a challenge, assuming, of course, that they have the tools and information they need to do so. In his book *Maslow on Management*, Abraham Maslow lists 19 assumptions that he suggests we should make of people. The four that are most relevant to this point are:

- Assume in all your people the impulse to achieve.

- Assume an active trend to self-actualization.

- Assume that people can take it, that they are tough, stronger than most people give them credit for.

- Assume that people are improvable.

In addition, we must remember that, generally speaking, the people with the greatest understanding and expertise in any given area are the people who are actually *doing* that work, and these people are not necessarily management. For an organization to achieve excellence, it must engage all of its organization members. Not only will these employees have the ability to engage, but most of them will have the desire to do so. Money is, of course, important, but the truth is that people rarely leave a company because of money. More often it is because they do not feel a part of the company and cannot see their contributions to it.

I have also discovered in my work that it really doesn't matter what an organization does; what matters is how purposeful it is at doing it. One of my favorite companies is Sashco Sealants, a company in the Denver area that manufactures caulking and other types of sealants. Not a particularly glamorous industry, but a truly beautiful organization. Unlike many organizations, that have their values, vision, and mission laminated and hanging on the wall (and, of course, none of their employees could tell you what they are), Sashco truly lives its stated values: truth, trust, caring, and forgiveness. It also has very high expectations of performance, however, and it has consistently performed at a much higher level than other organizations in its industry. Here are a few more examples of purposeful organizations I've had the privilege of working with:

- Onions, Etc., a produce distributor in Northern California, considers itself to be a servant to its customers. It believes that its main product is service, and it truly enjoys providing it (this is a common characteristic of purposeful organizations).

- The National Center for Employee Ownership, a nonprofit organization that provides information and resources to its members on the subject of ESOPs (Employee Stock Ownership Plans) and other broad-based equity programs, has a clear culture of trust and accountability and the mechanisms to support that. Employees will tell you that getting results is more important to them than satisfying the boss and that if someone doesn't fit this mold, that person doesn't last.

- HCSS, a software company in Houston that focuses on products for the construction industry, is also dedicated to the idea of service as its primary product. There is a high level of employee involvement at HCSS, and the company is very focused on lifelong learning. It also happens to be an ESOP company, with approximately 30 percent of its stock being owned by employees.

- The New Belgium Brewing Company (NBB) is another example of a purposeful company. As does HCSS (and frankly all of the purposeful and high performing companies I've worked with), New Belgium has a very high involvement culture, and in its case, every employee has input into the goals, objectives, and direction of the business. The company also happens to be very energy conscious and is nearly 100 percent energy self-sufficient.

Every one of these organizations, and hundreds more that I've had the honor to work with, have created purposeful and enjoyable cultures, are highly profitable, and retain employees at a significantly greater rate than their competitors who do not follow this path. And so, as I stated earlier, I don't believe that we are doomed to a future of entitlement. However, organizations and business leaders *must take action* in order to shake people out of their entitlement habits and set them on the path to achievement and true self-esteem. Ownership Thinking is the mechanism to accomplish that.

The Paradox of Altruism

Many of you may have noticed that I dedicated this book to Ayn Rand. I have done this primarily because of her book *Atlas Shrugged* and the tremendous impact it had on my life and work. It is a very complex book with many messages, but the message that speaks to me the most is the impact of misdirected altruism, the manipulative power it can create in the wrong hands, and the ultimate destruction it can wreak on a society. It's important to comment on this point now because it is critical to understand that we are not talking about a lack of caring here; in fact, quite the contrary is true.

There are people in the United States who need help, and some of them are unable to help themselves (this is far truer in other parts of the world). I do believe it is our obligation to help these people; however, *there really are not that many people in this condition.* The vast majority of people who are struggling have the capacity to help themselves. Misplaced altruism would be providing these people with a long-term handout and no requirement that they get back into the game (or on the path to do so). This, in fact, leads to dependence, which, as I've already noted, leads to feelings of purposelessness and misery. In addition, it forces everyone else to give up more and more toward feeding the habit of those who are now addicted to entitlement (which creates resentment).

19

Webster's definition of *altruism* is "unselfish interest in the welfare of others." This would imply giving to those in need. The question we must ask is: What can we give that will improve other people's lives in the long term and *our own* life as well? Our obligation is not to focus on the short-term fix but rather *to teach people how to become self-reliant*. And when they become self-reliant, it then becomes their obligation to teach others the same. This is a truly noble form of altruism.

I mentioned the terms *abundance* and *scarcity* earlier in this chapter. Abundant thinking is about recognizing that there is more available to us in life than we can possibly imagine. We must use the tools we are provided (in other words, the gifts we are given) to earn these things, which in turn provides us with purpose. We can then become even more purposeful by giving to others the ability we have found to become self-reliant. A pure body of water must have an inlet flowing into it and a spillway for water to exit. Without these, the body of water becomes stagnant. Scarcity thinking, on the other hand, is about fear: *I must have this. I must hold on to this. What if I lose this?* Scarcity thinking is fueled by misdirected altruism.

I had two events happen to me in the months prior to the publication of this book that I found very interesting and relevant to this discussion. The first occurred when I sent the manuscript out to several people whose names I had been given as people who might have an interest in representing the book to publishers for me (agents). As might be expected, a few people responded very positively and with great interest (one of whom I mention in the acknowledgments), a few were rather lukewarm, and a few did not respond at all. There was one, however, who was actually offended by my basic premise that entitlement is a significant issue that needs to be addressed. He said that he did not believe that people were entitled and spoiled (stating that I somehow implied that this was the nature of Americans), but were doing their best and were simply scared. I suspect that this is a person with a good heart, who wants to see people have the things they need to lead happy lives. He is also, in my opinion, a perfect example of misdirected altruism. I think this is a point that should be addressed.

It is not at all the nature of Americans (or people anywhere) to be entitled and spoiled. I believe the opposite is true. What makes America unique in the world is the work ethic and entrepreneurial spirit that has enabled us for generations to build something from nothing through effort and perseverance and to be an example of excellence in a world that is largely impoverished and dangerous. The point is that year after year we are creating more opportunities for people to be lulled into being taken care of and coddled, ultimately becoming entitled and purposeless. Again, people are drawn to security for obvious reasons, but I believe it saps the energy that made this country great and has previously created greatness in its citizens. In addition, people are ultimately not happy leading purposeless lives, and purposeless lives are a tragic waste of potential.

The second event occurred at a group I belong to that meets regularly to discuss spiritual matters and to grow in that regard. It is a wonderful group that I've been involved with for many years, and I have become very close to many of its members. One of these people is a woman who I would guess to be in her late sixties, and who I have come to love dearly. After our meeting one morning, she was telling me about a political issue that was ongoing at the time, obviously assuming that I would agree with her point of view. My view was, however, that she was really talking about misdirected altruism. When I pointed out that I disagreed with her and that my views were somewhat conservative in this regard, she said in all earnestness: "Oh! I assumed you would not come from that way of thinking, because I know that you do such good things for people." This is a perfect example of the paradox of altruism. The question is not *if* we give, but *what and how*.

Common Characteristics of Great Companies

Some time ago I was having dinner with a client of mine, who at one point during dinner asked me the following question: "You've worked with hundreds of companies, Brad. What are some of the common characteristics you see in the truly great ones?" As far as I could remember, no one had ever asked me this question before. Three characteristics came to mind immediately upon hearing the question, and I continue to see these three qualities in the best companies that I have worked with ever since.

The first characteristic I see in these companies is that *they care*. They care deeply. They care about one another, they care about their product or service, they care about their customers. But they typically care about something bigger. In other words, they have a higher purpose. At one of our Ownership Thinking annual conferences, I gave a talk on "spirituality in business," which addressed this common theme in great companies. I think this probably freaked out a few people when they saw it on the program, but what I mean by spirituality is simply purposefulness, getting out of self, and having the self-discipline to do so.

New Belgium Brewing is a good example of this. When you visit the company, you can feel the sense of family and love among the employees. In addition to caring about its employees and, of course, its customers, NBB is very community minded. One of its founders, Kim Jordan, was the keynote speaker at our 2008 conference, and rather than accepting a fee, she asked that we donate something to one of her favorite charities: a nonprofit that sponsors bike paths in her hometown of Fort Collins. NBB also sponsors a very popular bicycling event each year called the "Tour de Fat." Here's a blurb I found about this event on the Internet:

> Grab your bike and slip into your alter-ego because New Belgium's philanthropic cycling circus Tour de Fat is hitting the road for its seventh season! Costumes and decorated bikes reign supreme as the participants come for a casual ride, good music and entertainment, then stay, of course, for the beer. Amid the hoopla, Tour de Fat also raises money for local charities.

As I mentioned earlier, NBB also cares deeply about the environment, and due to its efforts in this area has become almost completely energy independent. It is the only company I'm aware of that has a Sustainability Coordinator, who is commonly referred to around the facility as the "Sustainability Goddess."

The second characteristic I see in the best companies is that *they have fun*. They recognize that employees spend a good deal of time at work, and it would probably be a good thing if they enjoyed being there. At Sashco, having fun is an integral part of the weekly forecasting meetings. Though the meetings are highly efficient and focused on business performance, you will find that noisemakers and toys (and celebrating wins) are part of the meetings as well. Sashco also owns a Chrysler Prowler, a very cool roadster that it has named The Cheetah Express. At the yearly performance incentive party (called the Big Cat Bash), the car is awarded for a year to the employee who has best met the following criteria:

- Must uphold Sashco's values of truth, trust, caring, and forgiveness; will practice these values by refraining from gossip, practicing self-control, and confronting issues with care

- Is willing to acknowledge mistakes

- Will have a positive attitude and will be a proactive learner, always furthering his or her education

- Must have been with Sashco for at least five years

- Contributes to the success of the team and Sashco

As you wander around the offices of HCSS, you will also see a lot of fun stuff. There are full-size cutouts of some of the employees' favorite movie characters and famous figures: Captain Kirk, Lara Croft (*Tomb Raider*), Snoopy on his doghouse, Dr. Evil, and Austin Powers, to name a few. You may see someone tooling around the office on the company Segway. Each month the company finances a birthday lunch for everyone who has a birthday that month. The company pays for registrations to events, such as triathlons, marathons, and bicycle races, and it is common for employees to train together for these events.

At NBB, employees receive a fat tire bicycle on their one-year anniversary. The bikes are unique each year (so you can tell when an employee started working there by the color and style of his or her bike) and are manufactured specifically for NBB. On their fifth year of employment at NBB, employees travel to Belgium for a weeklong bike tour, following in the footsteps of Kim Jordan and her husband, Jeff (cofounder of NBB), who spent time traveling around Belgium on bicycles learning about Belgium-style beer prior to starting the company.

Most of these employee benefits at Sashco, HCSS, and NBB require financial resources, which leads me to the third characteristic I see in the very best companies: *They have very high expectations of performance.* Performance is not measured by activity but rather by operational and financial excellence. Now this is an interesting mix of characteristics, and many people struggle with the idea of caring, fun, and high expectations of performance fitting in the same box. The reason they struggle with it is that, from their experience at other companies, high expectations of performance have come only from ownership and management. However, what you notice in the very best companies is that high expectations permeate the company—from bottom to top and across the organization. They simply have *winning cultures.* And so, not only is it possible to have an organization that cares, has fun, *and* is financially successful, I can tell you from my experience that the companies that are purposeful and fun are quite often *the most* financially successful.

People

Another great benefit of practicing the principles and activities outlined in this book is that you will create an *organization* of excellence rather than *pockets* of excellence. By following this path, you will create an organization of very high visibility and high accountability. This is largely because people simply cannot hide. There is a certain type of individual who really can't tolerate high visibility. As you may have guessed, these are typically your poorest performers (and I have found this often goes hand in hand with poor attitudes). They are the people who have learned how to hide, and they often hide in "busyness." Once the spotlight of results is shone on them, these people either rise to the occasion or simply go away. In this environment, their peers will generally help them to do one or the other. In an environment of high visibility, where everyone is benefiting from the success of the organization or suffering from poor organizational performance, peers become less tolerant of poor performance and behavior. It becomes something of a self-selecting environment. Given this, you may lose a few people when you begin practicing Ownership Thinking in your organization, but I can assure you that they will be the people you want to lose. In the long run, companies that practice the Ownership Thinking way of doing business retain employees at a rate 200 percent higher than that of companies that don't. This can be attributed to the fact that these companies are simply better places to work. Obviously, this won't hurt as it relates to recruiting either. I know of many companies doing business this way that have a great supply of high-quality candidates waiting in the wings. As an example, I was speaking to a flight attendant on a recent Southwest flight who was telling me that Southwest recently had over 200,000 applicants for 180 available flight attendant positions. I was not able to verify the numbers, but I did find this in the February 14, 2011, issue of the *Dallas Morning News*:

> A flood of job applicants, trying to get into Southwest's website to seek flight attendant positions Monday, overwhelmed the company's servers, preventing many hopefuls from being able to submit applications during the two-hour window that the Dallas-based carrier allowed online applications.

Ownership Thinking is also a terrific employee development tool. In this environment, employees are not simply learning the tasks required of their position. They become active participants in the business of the business and begin to understand the impact of their work on other individuals and departments and on the financial performance of the organization. I have a video that was sent to me by one of my clients some time ago that highlights this point (it is available to view from our Web site home page—www.ownershipthinking.com). The video was made by the head of the client's Ownership Thinking Steering Committee (see Chapter 7) and simply shows a variety of employees throughout the company discussing the Rapid Improvement Plans (Chapter 5) they had been involved in. This is a 2,000-person manufacturing company in rural Georgia, and the employees are discussing (in great detail and with obvious clarity and understanding) the financial impact they have had on the organization because of their efforts. This understanding of the interactions between departments, and the financial ramifications of their decisions, clearly adds to the value these individuals can bring to the organization and allows them to grow into more significant roles. A specific example of this growth, and one that I'm particularly proud of, is my administrative assistant at MFD de México (Leonor Leon), who went on to run that company as its president when I finished my contract and returned to the United States.

I was having a conversation with one of my long-term clients recently, and he was telling me about the impact of Ownership Thinking on the quality of his personnel. One of his employees, someone who had been doing very good work, had left for another opportunity. After about six months, he was back, asking if he could return. Many business owners or leaders would probably not consider rehiring such a person (pride or ego, I suppose), but my client was delighted to do so. He knew not only that the employee was a solid worker but also that, after seeing that the grass was not so green on the other side, the employee would now be an enthusiastic champion of the company's culture when communicating with other employees, and of course with the community at large. Evidently this was not the first time that someone had left the company and wanted to come back.

Here is a final note on people. Don't do what most companies do, which is to hire quickly and fire slowly. When making a hire, take your time to ensure that you have the right person, not only from a technical standpoint, but also in terms of attitude.

Skills can usually be taught, but my experience tells me that attitudes and behaviors are pretty tough to change. I have seen many organizations have success by allowing team members to participate in the interview process of a candidate who would ultimately be working in their area if hired. I'm also a firm believer in using assessment tools (such as those offered by my friend Lloyd Gottman of Synergetic Systems) when making a hire. These assessments typically don't require a significant investment, particularly when you look at the tremendous cost and disruption created by a poor hire.

Perhaps most important, if you make a bad hire and the person obviously does not fit the culture or possess the abilities necessary to be successful, make that determination as quickly as possible and cut the cord. Business leaders often agonize over making the decision to terminate someone, because it is painful to do so. It's painful for two reasons. First, it typically makes it clear that they made a mistake in hiring and now have to admit it. And second, it is difficult to terminate someone knowing the impact it will have not only on the person but also on his or her family. When leaders finally get up the nerve to let someone go, the rest of the employees will probably think, "What took you so long?" Aside from the damage that this person has done to the organization, consider the damage done to the leaders' credibility. Delaying the inevitable is also profoundly unfair to everyone else in the organization, whose financial well-being and job security are now tied to its performance.

The Financial Benefits of Ownership Thinking

Now that we've looked at the various moral, ethical, and developmental reasons for practicing Ownership Thinking, let's look at the financial benefits. You may be thinking: "Where's the beef?" In other words, what kind of measurable financial results might you expect by going down this path?

I mentioned in the Introduction to this book that we more than doubled our profitability in the first year of practicing Ownership Thinking at MFD. This is far from being an anomaly. I have seen similar (or better) results in dozens of companies since 1995, and very significant results in hundreds more. Let's take a look at four examples.

OFFICE ENVIRONMENTS AND SERVICES

An office furniture distributor with roughly $10 million in annual revenue at the time it implemented Ownership Thinking ($17 million today), Office Environments and Services saw the following results in its first year of practicing Ownership Thinking:

- It went from a $395k loss to a profit of $650k, which reflected a $1,045,000 turnaround in one year. It should be noted that this represents a profit of over 6 percent in an industry that averages about 3 percent.

30

■ It went from a $500k negative cash flow to a $360k positive cash flow.

■ Average collection days went from 50 to 29.

■ Inventory turns went from 15 to (incredibly) 65.

■ Employees averaged $3,300 each in incentive payouts (the employees had never had an incentive plan before).

SYNTHETIC INDUSTRIES

Synthetic Industries, a $500 million manufacturer, had a 15 percent increase in EBITDA in its second year by accomplishing the following with Ownership Thinking:

■ Off-quality product was reduced to 2.4 percent from over 5 percent.

■ Extrusion waste was reduced to 3.6 percent from 4 percent.

■ Quality improvements accounted for over $2 million in cost savings.

■ Inventory value was reduced by over $30 million.

■ Turnover was reduced by 40 percent.

- Safety enhancements reduced workers compensation expense by $1.1. million.

STEVE WINTER, CEO OF ERGOS TECHNOLOGY

Steve Winter is the CEO of ERGOS Technology, based in Houston. He sent me the following testimonial in 2009:

> I was introduced to Ownership Thinking through another extremely happy client just prior to the end of 2007. I was looking for a way to boost profits and provide a way for our employees to share in the fruits of their labor. I contacted Brad and he came to our offices in December 2007, and on January 1, 2008, we implemented Ownership Thinking. In 2008 we tripled our bottom line and distributed over $300K in profits to our employees! Pretty miraculous results. Ownership Thinking was the best investment we have ever made, and it only took a few days to learn this incredible process.

NATE KOLENSKI, CEO OF BLOCKTOPS

Blocktops is a company that specializes in the custom design, fabrication, and installation of high-end stone, wood, and solid surface products. CEO Nate Kolenski sent me the following note in 2010:

> I was introduced to Ownership Thinking by a colleague who had used the program with great success. We had always worked to include our management team in plan-

ning, budgeting, and goal setting but had challenges getting the information to the rest of the staff. Without accurate information and knowledge, bonuses and incentives were looked at as either a pleasant surprise or an entitlement.

After we completed the Ownership Thinking training of our management team and staff we set the date and had a company-wide kick-off meeting. The day following our launch we unexpectedly received news that would reduce our business revenue by nearly 70 percent. The Ownership Thinking training our people received in forecasting and reducing waste and expenses prepared us for the massive change in revenue. It was a key part of our profitability and even survival during the setback and economic downturn that followed over the next two years. We are now positioned for growth and have funded our incentive for two consecutive quarters—largely because we adopted and implemented the Ownership Thinking philosophy and tools at just the right time.

How confident am I that you will see significant financial benefits? I am confident enough to guarantee our clients a return on their investment with us in 90 days, or we will refund their fee. After implementing this in over 1,000 companies, we have yet to have one of them ask for a refund. Here is something to consider: the average amount of unrealized profit (we call this, profit that is "falling through the cracks") in small to medium-sized companies, and across all industries, is approximately 8 percent. When you look at the figures I noted in the examples, it is easy to see why. An important thing to remember is that this is not occurring because employees don't care or don't want to contribute. Quite the contrary is true. The issue is simply that they have not been taught where the cracks are and why they are there, nor given the tools, training, and information to close them up.

Share the Insomnia

As I've pointed out in this chapter, there are many reasons for practicing Ownership Thinking and many benefits as well. Since you are a business owner or leader, I would ask you to consider one more. How great would it be if all of your employees thought about the business as you do? What if they had the knowledge and sense of ownership to consider the financial ramifications of their decisions? What if they were able to visualize the impact of the decisions they made in their area on other areas in the company? What if they worried about (or at least concerned themselves with) economic conditions, the competition, and risk—and factored these considerations into their decisions and actions? What if they thought and acted in a manner that was first and foremost in the best interest of the company? Practicing Ownership Thinking will allow you, as an owner or a leader, to rest easier knowing that your employees are making decisions and taking actions that are aligned with what you would do yourself. In addition to the peace of mind this obviously brings, it will allow you to focus on those things that you enjoy the most and are the best at doing. Zimmerman Boulos, the owner and CEO of Office Environments and Services, once told me that, although the financial benefits of practicing Ownership Thinking were great, the most important benefit for him personally was that it made being the CEO "fun again."

KEY CONCEPTS

- Entitlement has become more and more pervasive in our culture over the past few generations. It not only damages our economy and organizational productivity, but, ironically, it destroys self-esteem.

- Ownership Thinking will help to eradicate the entitlement mentality in your organization and replace it with a mentality of earning.

- It doesn't matter what an organization does, what matters is how it does it. Any organization in any industry can practice Ownership Thinking.

- The three common characteristics in the best companies are (1) they care, (2) they have fun, and (3) they have very high expectations of performance.

- People are the foundation of any great company. Ownership Thinking will help to attract the best people and will create an environment where peers will not tolerate poor performers.

- Organizations that practice Ownership Thinking are market leaders and financially far more successful than companies that do not practice it.

- Roughly 8 percent of potential profit may be falling through the cracks in your company, and your employees can help you to recover it.

- As a business owner or leader, Ownership Thinking will help you to "share the insomnia" with your employees and probably enjoy your work and life more.

CHAPTER TWO

How to Create Incentive Plans . . . That Work!

igure 2.1 represents the four components of Ownership Thinking: The Right People, The Right Education, The Right Measures, and The Right Incentives. I have not dedicated a chapter to The Right People in this book but rather talk about it throughout because, unlike the other three components that have defined strategies, The Right People is mostly an outcome of practicing Ownership Thinking. However, I do provide some feedback and advice as it relates to hiring and retaining the best people. I also suggest that you read Marcus Buckingham and Curt Coffman's book, *First, Break All the Rules*. It is by far the best book I've read on the subject of talent: how to find it, hire it, retain it, and develop it.

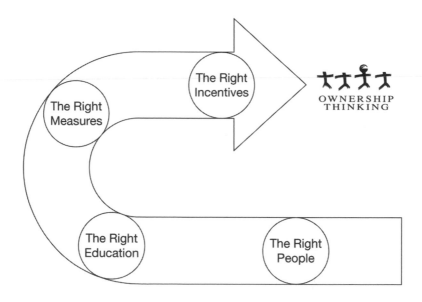

FIGURE 2.1

Although The Right Incentives is actually the last component of the Ownership Thinking model (Figure 2.1), I will discuss it early in this book for the following two reasons.

The first reason is that it tends to be the hottest topic for both employees and management. From an employee perspective, it is the WIIFM (What's In It For Me) piece, and therefore, at least initially, the most interesting component of the model. From a management perspective, many, if not most, incentive plans today don't work very well, and this creates a good deal of frustration (and also cynicism) on the part of business owners and managers, which makes them hungry to see something that can alleviate that frustration.

The second reason is probably more important. When I do speeches or workshops on Ownership Thinking, I historically end those talks with the subject of incentives because it is the fourth and last component of our model. After the presentation is over, many people leave with the idea that Ownership Thinking is primarily about incentive plans because I talk about it last. However, this assumption is wrong. In order to have a successful incentive plan, you must do work in the other three components (which we will be discussing). If you shortchange the first three components, you are highly unlikely to generate the additional profit and cash in your company to support the incentive plan. This leads to the most important thing to remember about incentive plans: *They must be self-funding.*

An Incentive Plan
Must Be Self-Funding

For an incentive plan to be self-funding, it must pay for itself. If your plan does not pay for itself, then what you've created is simply a new expense. You've also created an entitlement (or, as someone attending one of my talks so aptly put it, you've created welfare). Given this, it is important to provide your employees with the education, measures, information, and tools outlined in this book to ensure that they find the money to fund the plan. If employees are going to be given the opportunity to participate in an incentive plan, then it is their obligation and responsibility to fund it. It follows, however, that it is the obligation of ownership and leadership to teach them how to do that and to provide them with the tools and training necessary to accomplish the task.

I have found that many (if not most) business owners and leaders look at incentives as if they were budgeted expenses, which can curtail their enthusiasm about creating them. I suggest you think of it this way instead: by implementing the Ownership Thinking way of doing business, profitability will increase from X to Y, and Y should be substantially greater than X. The organization now has additional profit dollars that are represented by the gap between X and Y, and the incentive will be a portion of that gap. In other words, the incentive is not only self-funded, but it will also drive the profitability of the organization higher, even after the incentive payout is made. *Everyone* must understand this simple premise: the incentive plan is meant to improve the financial performance of the company and to shape employee behavior accordingly. Incentives should never be paid if financial performance does not warrant them.

I should also point out some precautions as they relate to your choice of words when creating and communicating your incentive plan to your employees. First, I'm not a big fan of the word *bonus*. There are a variety of definitions out there for the word, but here is a typical one: "Something given or paid in addition to what is usual or expected." The key word in this sentence is *given*, which infers a gift or a freebee. On the other hand, Webster defines the word *incentive* as follows: "Something that incites or is likely to incite to determination or action." An incentive, or incentive plan, therefore, is provided on the condition of a behavioral change and a positive, measurable outcome to that behavior. As I stated in the Introduction, an incentive plan should shape employee behavior toward improving financial performance. Try to use the word *opportunity* whenever you are describing an incentive plan to employees, which should emphasize that incentives must be earned through specific performance requirements above and beyond the standard job description. An incentive plan is an opportunity to create more personal wealth, and it is not to be considered a compensation.

In this chapter, I will provide you with both the elements of well-designed incentive plans and the specifics of poorly designed incentive plans to ensure that you do not make any common mistakes. Additionally, I'll give you detailed information and examples, based on my company's extensive experience, of how to design a successful plan for your company.

Elements of Poorly Designed Incentive Plans

Prior to starting my consulting practice, I noticed that most incentive plans I'd seen did not work, and (as I pointed out in the Introduction) many actually caused damage to the organization. So when I started Ownership Thinking in the mid-nineties, I did some research on what mistakes companies make when designing their incentive plans. I found the following to be common flaws:

- The plan creates separate fiefdoms.

- The plan is discretionary.

- Employees think that (true or not) the goals are unrealistic or unattainable.

- The payout opportunity is too small—there is no perceived value.

- The goals of the plan are not communicated, so employees cannot see the connection between the work that they do and the incentive payouts they receive.

- The goals of the plan change during the communicated time frame of the plan.

SEPARATE FIEFDOMS

When business owners and leaders set out to create an incentive plan, many start with the underlying idea that if they just create the right plan, it will manage their people. This line of thought *seems* logical: that incentives should be tailored to individuals or groups and that if a department or individual is required to do X, Y, and Z, then an incentive plan should be created that is tied to the performance of X, Y, and Z. More often than not, however, X, Y, and Z are not financially quantifiable. The owners will then go through the same exercise with each of the other departments or individuals throughout the organization. As you might imagine, the result is a ridiculously complex set of incentives that is universally not understood (and therefore not trusted) by employees and is a nightmare to administer. Most important, a distinct disadvantage of these multiple incentive plans is that the leaders have now created a situation where each department or individual is being motivated to look out for his or her own best interest rather than the best interest of the organization as a whole. As a result, it is conceivable that members from one department might sabotage other departments to ensure that their department meets its goals and that they receive their incentives.

Let's look at an example. I had worked with a $70 million construction company that was significantly underperforming. It had multiple incentive plans in place, but one region was consistently receiving incentive rewards while the other regions were not. I discovered that the manager of the region winning the incentive rewards was hoarding all of the best equipment (even equipment not being used at the time) and all of the best people toward ensuring he met his goals. Obviously, the rest of the company was suffering from these actions.

Another disadvantage of multiple plans is that there is no assurance that the company will be profitable, even if some departments or individuals are receiving incentive payouts. Finally, it is virtually impossible to create multiple plans and remain objective. If managers are to determine who will be receiving an incentive payout and who will not, they will quite often give the incentives to the people they simply like the best. This, of course, raises questions of fairness and can damage morale.

I should point out that sales departments must be treated differently (in most cases), and the marketplace often demands this. Commissions are fine, as long as they are properly designed, meaning that they are not just about revenue. I've always considered the role of a salesperson to be a "champion of margin"—it's not just about bringing revenue to the table, but instead, *profitable revenue*. The absolute worst scenario I have encountered is a salesperson who is commissioned on revenue and has the ability to negotiate or manipulate pricing. In this case, the company is just asking for reduced margins. Keeping this in mind, I suggest you set up one of the following scenarios: (1) salespeople are commissioned on revenue, and pricing is engraved in stone, or (2) salespeople can negotiate pricing and are commissioned on margin. If you chose the latter, it's critical that you teach the sales team members everything they need to know about margins and that they have a sliding commission scale allowing them to do better if they bring higher margin sales to the table.

The remaining question, then, is whether your salespeople will also participate in the broad-based plan. Generally, I would say yes because you want them to be thinking about overall company performance, not simply about their little world of sales. When I discuss distribution methods later in the chapter, I will touch on this again.

DISCRETIONARY INCENTIVES

Your company has had a pretty good year, and there is a little money left in the checking account at year-end. So, probably at Christmastime, you hand out checks to everyone. Yea! This might make you feel good (it is somewhat patriarchal), and it will probably make your employees feel good for the moment. However, all you've really given them is a gift. Remember, the purpose of an incentive plan is to shape employee behavior toward improving the financial performance of the company. The gift you gave them is not tied to behavior and therefore will not change behavior— until perhaps they don't get one! Once again, you have created an entitlement.

UNREALISTIC (OR PERCEIVED UNREALISTIC) GOALS

When I was working with the office furniture distributor (see the Introduction), they had just finished a very tough year (roughly $9 million in revenue and a $395k loss). After working with the leadership team to identify their Key Performance Indicators, I met with both the leaders and the employees to determine where money had been falling through the cracks. We determined that a budget for next year of $11 million in revenue and a profit of $550k (5 percent) was doable as a stretch goal. The employees bought into this

45

stretch goal because they saw where the cracks were and became a part of the plan to seal them up. Here are a few of those cracks:

- Poor labor efficiency due to lack of job costing

- Sales team focus on revenue rather than margin (discounting quotes, making concessions, and so on)

- A lack of emphasis on service sales (rather than product sales), which were generally more profitable

- Excessive punch list items requiring follow-up work without the ability to invoice

- Errors in order entry: finish, fabric, pricing, and so on

- Installation damage and concealed damage on receipt of product

- Excessive nonbillable overtime

- High average collection days

- Small-tool loss and damage

Imagine if none of this work had been done with the leadership or employees, and the owner of the company had simply come up with this budget by himself, in a vacuum, so to speak. As an employee, how would you feel about that budget, knowing that you had just finished a losing year? Of course, you wouldn't buy into it, and most likely you would think the owner was dreaming (or out of his mind). The point is that employees bought into this stretch goal because they were actively involved in identifying the money falling through the cracks and agreed that these areas could be improved by using Ownership Thinking. This company actually exceeded the stretch goal in its first year of practicing Ownership Thinking. The moral is: it's not only whether the budget is realistic or not that's important, but also that your employees *believe in it*.

NO PERCEIVED VALUE

An incentive opportunity of $10 a year is probably not going to motivate people (in fact, it most likely will irritate them), but an incentive opportunity of 10 percent of their salary is something quite different. In other words, the incentive opportunity (once the stretch goal has been met) should be enough to get employees' attention. Be sure that it is always clear that the incentive must be self-funded. I will discuss this in more detail later in this chapter when we look at plan design.

GOALS ARE NOT COMMUNICATED

One of the biggest problems with the majority of incentive plans is that a very weak link (or no link at all) exists between the work that employees are doing and the incentives payouts they are receiving (or not). If the goal of the plan is to shape behavior, which, as you now know, it should be, then it is critical for employees to have a clear understanding of the goals that have been set for the plan.

If the plan is based on Profit Before Tax (PBT), they must know what the threshold is, what the stretch goal is, what the payout opportunity is after the threshold, and so on. Just as important, they must know what Key Performance Indicators (KPIs) need to be focused on in order to find the money to fund the plan, and they must have the tools and information to become active participants in driving those KPIs. If this link is not clearly made, and if employees are not active participants, then, once again, the plan will become an entitlement plan. This will be discussed in greater detail in Chapters 3 and 4 (see the discussion of KPIs and Rapid Improvement Plans).

CHANGING THE PLAN

Most incentive plans (the ones we design, at any rate) are tied to projected annual PBT performance and chunked into quarterly opportunities (more on this later). Once designed, the plan should be communicated to your employees, along with key areas of focus to ensure that the plan will be funded. I suggest that you reevaluate your incentive plan every year as you go through your budgeting process, as it is likely that you will tweak it from year to year. The design may stay fundamentally the same, but the numbers will change based on revenue growth, improvements in operational efficiencies, changes in product or client strategy, and so on. When you introduce the plan each year, communicate clearly to employees that this is the plan for the upcoming year, but that there is no guarantee that it will remain the same in subsequent years. Also, I strongly advise you not to make *any* changes to the plan during the year for which it has been designed.

I've seen two different scenarios here. In the first, the organization comes out of the gate very strongly and (for example) may have two great quarters with substantial incentive payouts. Leadership may become anxious about the size of the incentive payouts (even though the plan is self-funded) and decide to raise the targets for the remainder of the year. Obviously, the credibility of the plan will be shot. Employees will not forget this, either, and it may take several years before they regain trust in the incentive plan (or in the leadership). In the second scenario, the company comes up a little short on its goals. However, the owners want to be nice, and since everyone has been so "busy," they decide to pay out an incentive anyway. The credibility of this plan has been shot as well. Moreover, the message sent to employees is that it doesn't really matter if they hit the goals or not. Once again, you have an entitlement plan.

Elements of Well-Designed Incentive Plans

Below are the elements of well-designed plans (based on our experience) that we design into our clients' plans:

- They are self-funding, and they ensure financial and value enhancements to the business.

- They have perceived value.

- They have shared targets.

- The goals are understandable.

- The goals are a stretch, but attainable.

- They clearly align employee behavior to business objectives.

SELF-FUNDING

From a financial perspective, the most important aspect of an incentive plan is that it pay for itself and that it add value to the organization. If you base your plan on PBT, you must first determine a minimum acceptable threshold of PBT before which no incentive will be paid. A common retort I get from employees is: "If the incentive is based on PBT, and all expenses are covered, why not begin paying out an incentive from dollar one of PBT?" First of all, all expenses have not been covered if the incentive is based on PBT. The expense that has not been addressed is the big T (Tax). This is no small chunk of change either, and you should inform your employees that businesses typically pay 40 percent of profit in taxes. Also, there are other organizational needs that must be considered beyond expenses. Businesses need capital for investments or improvements (such as equipment, which is capitalized rather than expensed), debt retirement, and return on investment for the shareholders. In addition, some industries have needs that are unique to them, such as bonding in the construction industry. By addressing all of these needs, you will arrive at a minimum threshold of profit that ensures that the company has the capital it needs to operate effectively and meet its growth objectives before any incentive considerations are made. The percentage share beyond this threshold should then allow for the organization to retain a reasonable level of profit after incentives are distributed.

PERCEIVED VALUE

In a poorly designed plan, an annual incentive opportunity of $10 is not going to do much to motivate your employees, but I have found that an incentive opportunity of 8 to 12 percent of wages will really get employees' attention. There is nothing particularly scientific about that range; it is just based on my experience. The question then becomes how to create an incentive opportunity in this range and still ensure that the plan meets your objectives. The steps I suggest are as follows:

- Determine your threshold as described above.

- Determine a realistic stretch goal. This number is not just snatched out of the air. It should be based on historical performance plus additional profit expectations from your focus on the KPIs that have been identified and the Rapid Improvement Plans that will be put into place to drive them (Chapters 3 and 4).

- Identify the budgeted payroll dollars for the year in question (compensation only—no taxes, commissions, or benefits).

51

Once these have been identified, you can identify a percentage of profit to share with your employees that will meet the 8 to 12 percent payout criterion once the stretch goal has been achieved. As an example, if the minimum threshold is $500k and the stretch goal is $800k, the gap between these is $300k. If the payroll budget is $1.2 million, and it is your goal to have a 10 percent incentive opportunity at the stretch goal, then the percentage of profit that should go toward the incentive pool after meeting the threshold is 40 percent (40 percent of $300k is $120k, or 10 percent of the total payroll; see Table 2.1).

TABLE 2.1

PBT After Payout	PBT	Incentive Pool (40%)
$500,000	$500,000	$0
$530,000	$550,000	$20,000
$560,000	$600,000	$40,000
$590,000	$650,000	$60,000
$620,000	$700,000	$80,000
$650,000	$750,000	$100,000
$680,000	$800,000	$120,000
$710,000	$850,000	$140,000
$740,000	$900,000	$160,000
$770,000	$950,000	$180,000
$800,000	$1,000,000	$200,000

Although the incentive payout objective is 8 to 12 percent of wages if the stretch goal is reached, this may not be realistic in every situation. I sometimes work with companies that have been marginally profitable for some time (due to performance rather than industry limitations). It is most likely unrealistic to draft a plan that assumes they will move from a break-even or loss position to a significant profit in year one. In this situation, the incentive opportunity at the stretch goal may be something significantly less than 8 to 12 percent—perhaps 3 or 4 percent. More often than not, these companies have not been paying incentives (shame on them if they have), and so anything is better than nothing. By practicing Ownership Thinking, they should be able to get their profitability up to a level that will allow for a more interesting incentive opportunity after a couple of years. Also, there are industries that simply have low profit margins by design (or due to the commoditized nature of the industry). Companies in these industries (distribution, for example), may never be able to provide incentive opportunities in the 8 to 12 percent range. Given industry limitations, it is assumed that their competitors will not be able to do so either.

SHARED TARGETS

As I mentioned previously in my discussion of "separate fiefdoms," there are several reasons to avoid creating an incentive plan that is tied to departmental or individual goals. The ultimate objective should always be to meet or exceed the profitability goal of the organization. This is not to say that incentives will be distributed equally to all employees (though they might be), but simply that the incentive *pool* will be based on the performance of the company versus the performance of any one department or individual. Everyone in the organization should be focused on this objective.

UNDERSTANDABLE GOALS

One of the reasons I suggest PBT as the driver of your incentive is that it is fairly easy to understand. Simply stated, it is the company's revenue less its expenses (all expenses excluding tax). Another reason is that every employee in the organization can impact PBT in one way or another (they just need to be taught how). I've seen companies base their incentive plans on EBITDA, for example, which is Earnings Before Interest, Taxes, Depreciation, and Amortization. Others have based theirs on EVA (Economic Value Added) or ROC (Return On Capital). In each of these cases, employees' eyes will likely glaze over when the plan is communicated to them. Once again, if they do not understand what drives the plan, it will have little or no impact on their behavior, and they probably will not trust it.

THE GOALS ARE A STRETCH, BUT ATTAINABLE

Employees must believe that the goals are attainable, though it should be clear that improved financial performance is required to fund the plan. As I mentioned earlier, quite often the issue isn't whether the goals are achievable but rather that employees are receiving all of the information and tools they need to recognize and find the money that has been "falling through the cracks." If you use all of the tools outlined in this book, the financial performance of your organization will increase significantly. Employees will often be skeptical of this at the outset. However, seeing is believing, and they will gain enthusiasm as they see improvements and how their contributions help advance those improvements.

EMPLOYEE BEHAVIOR ALIGNED WITH BUSINESS OBJECTIVES

The fundamental premise of Ownership Thinking is to create cultures of employees who think and act like owners toward creating wealth. Given this, all of the tools outlined in this book are designed to align employee behavior with the financial, operational, and strategic objectives of the business. If the desired result of your incentive plan is to increase the profitability of your organization, then the plan must be tied to the profitability of the organization. Frankly, this is the simple part. In the remaining chapters you will learn how to actively involve your employees in driving profitability and how to do so in an efficient, transparent, enjoyable, and mature fashion.

Designing Your Plan

Now that you are familiar with the elements of poorly designed incentive plans as opposed to well-designed incentive plans, the design elements should make a good deal of sense to you. Here are 10 questions you must answer in order to design your plan:

1. What is the key indicator that will drive the plan (or in a few cases, two key indicators)?

2. Who will participate?

3. What is your threshold?

4. What is your stretch goal?

5. What is your total payroll? Number of employees?

6. What is your percentage share (to get to an incentive payout of roughly 10 percent at the stretch goal)?

7. Should your plan be capped with a maximum payout? If so, what is it and why?

8. What is your distribution method?

9. Should the plan be quarterly, annual, or something else?

10. Should there be a separate management pool?

KEY INDICATORS

Almost all of the plans my company designs are tied to PBT. Again, this is the score that your employees can impact (most cannot impact tax). On rare occasions, you might need a second key indicator that drives cash flow. For example, one of my clients, roughly a $10 million company, had a history of collection problems. The company was in a particularly uncomfortable situation—it had to pay out an incentive because it met its profitability goal, but it did not have the cash to pay it. So what could the company do? What would you do? Borrow money to pay the incentive? Ouch. For this company, then, the incentive was tied to PBT, but there was a caveat tied to average collection days (Accounts Receivables [AR]): If the company was at 45 average collection days or less at the date of incentive distribution, then the entire incentive was paid. From 45 to 50 average collection days, the payout was 50 percent, and if it was at 50 days or more, there was no payout.

This offered an opportunity to teach employees about another aspect of the business, which was AR. If you are thinking that this is not fair because AR can only be impacted by the accounting department, you will learn that this is not true in Chapter 5.

PARTICIPANTS

In nearly every case, I strongly advise my clients that everyone should participate in the incentive plan, which is why I call them *broad-based plans* (however this does not infer that the incentive pool will be equally distributed). Keep this in mind: everyone can contribute to the financial performance of the company, and everyone can sabotage it. As I have said before, we want to create organizations of excellence, not pockets of excellence.

If you determine that the plan will be broad based, then the question is no longer "who will participate" but rather *"how do they participate?"* I will answer this question a little later in my discussion of distribution methods and separate management pools. On rare occasions, I have come across an organization where it didn't necessarily make sense to include everyone in the incentive plan. Typically, it will be a company that exhibits one or more of these characteristics:

- The laborers are somewhat transient, and/or the business is highly seasonal and employs a number of temporary workers.

- The incentive for laborers is overtime.

- It is a union shop.

Regarding the last point, unions are often not very receptive to any type of pay-for-performance plan, so they may be difficult to sell on the idea. It's a pity because I've always believed that unions should work to ensure the following for their members: (1) competitive wages, (2) a safe environment, and (3) security. From my experience, there is no better way to achieve these things for employees than by practicing Ownership Thinking. If you want to include your union, I suggest that you approach it from that angle. If you can sell your union on the idea, then it becomes quite easy to implement the program with its support. I once worked with a division of Alcoa that was able to engage its union, and the outcome was fascinating. Not only was there a tremendous amount of buy-in and performance enhancements (both operational and financial), but union member grievances virtually disappeared.

DETERMINING THRESHOLD

Every organization will have financial needs (capital needs) beyond just its expenses. These will typically include, but not necessarily be limited to, Return On Investment (ROI) for shareholders, debt retirement, and capital for improvements or investments. Some of these may actually be dictated by bank covenants. Depending on the structure of your business, you must consider tax as well (assuming the incentive is based on PBT). Your threshold is the amount of profit required to address these financial needs of the company. No incentive will be paid until the company is trending to meet this threshold. I'll explain how to calculate this a bit later.

STRETCH GOALS

I define a stretch goal as the profit number that can be reached if a company is utilizing the Ownership Thinking tools and principles effectively, and is "firing on all cylinders." The stretch goal can be determined by examining the following:

- What has the historical performance of the company been?

- What does your budget look like for the coming year?

- What kind of money do you think has been falling through the cracks?

To determine the stretch goal, first go through the Rapid Improvement Plan Exercise, as outlined in Chapter 5, for those areas that can be addressed realistically in the upcoming incentive year. The stretch goal may also be affected by some of the action items that come out of your Key Indicator Workshop (Chapter 4) as well as by the Key Indicators that come out of the workshop (see the office furniture distributor example of unrealistic goals provided earlier in this chapter).

TOTAL PAYROLL AND NUMBER OF EMPLOYEES

You will need the total payroll number (wages only, excluding taxes, benefits, incentives, and commissions) to help determine what percentage of PBT, after your threshold, will be going into the incentive pool. Again, an incentive pool that is 8 to 12 percent of total wages at your stretch goal is ideal, but not always realistic. By playing around with the percentage share, you can determine what would be necessary to achieve this number. I rarely suggest a number higher than 40 percent; however I occasionally build a plan with a 50 percent share after threshold.

The total number of employees (or full-time equivalents) is only needed if you will be distributing the plan equally. You will need that number to create a spreadsheet showing the payout schedule at different levels of profitability. An example of this is shown in Table 2.2. The row that is highlighted is the stretch goal.

PERCENTAGE SHARE

This is the percentage of profit after the minimum threshold that will be funding the incentive plan. I have already discussed this in some detail; however there is one more design element that you

TABLE 2.2

Incentive Pool	Q1 (50% Held)	Q2 (50% held)	Q3 (50% Held)	Q4 Total Adjusted	Total	X75 Employees
$0	$0	$0	$0	$0	$0	$0
$40,000	$67	$67	$67	$333	$533	$40,000
$80,000	$133	$133	$133	$667	$1,067	$80,000
$120,000	$200	$200	$200	$1,000	$1,600	$120,000
$160,000	$267	$267	$267	$1,333	$2,133	$160,000
$200,000	$333	$333	$333	$1,667	$2,667	$200,000
$240,000	$400	$400	$400	$2,000	$3,200	$240,000
$280,000	$467	$467	$467	$2,333	$3,733	$280,000
$320,000	$533	$533	$533	$2,667	$4,267	$320,000
$360,000	$600	$600	$600	$3,000	$4,800	$360,000
$400,000	$667	$667	$667	$3,333	$5,333	$400,000
$425,000	$1,700	$3,400	$5,100	$6,800	$17,000	$425,000
$450,000	$1,800	$3,600	$5,400	$7,200	$18,000	$450,000
$475,000	$1,900	$3,800	$5,700	$7,600	$19,000	$475,000
$500,000	$2,000	$4,000	$6,000	$8,000	$20,000	$500,000

might want to consider. If you have an organization that has been marginally profitable in previous years, yet you wish to have a plan that would offer some payout even at a level that does not meet your long-term goals (or industry standards, perhaps), you can create a plan with escalating payouts. For example, 20 percent of PBT after a minimum threshold of X will go to the incentive pool, 30 percent of PBT after exceeding milestone Y, and 40 percent of PBT after exceeding milestone Z.

SHOULD THE PLAN HAVE A CAP, AND IF SO, WHAT SHOULD IT BE?

By capping the plan, I mean identifying a maximum incentive payout opportunity. For example, an organization may decide to cap the incentive at 15 percent of total wages. Once this payout has been achieved, any further profit will not allow for a contribution to the plan. As you might expect, if the maximum payout has been achieved, some steam may come out of the plan. Therefore, I *generally* do not suggest doing this. However, keep in mind that the plan is self-funding and that by following the guidelines and principles outlined in this book, your employees will be active participants in funding the plan. I do suggest capping the plan in a few situations and have noted them below.

- **In companies with an Employee Stock Option Plan (ESOP) or some other form of broad-based equity sharing plan.** In these organizations, PBT is no longer the "score at the end of the game." The endgame is now stock value. These organizations must focus more on retained earnings, and building a strong balance sheet will help toward this end. In addition, many ESOPs are highly leveraged (because they take on debt to make the transaction), and so additional cash is needed to retire the debt.

- **In nonprofit organizations.** It may seem counterintuitive, but you can have an incentive plan tied to profit in nonprofits, although the driver will not be called profit but rather something like Net Operating Income or Net Reserves. Incentive plans in these instances must be capped, because if the organization is audited and it is deemed that employees are receiving "unreasonable compensation," the organization can lose its nonprofit status.

- **In industries that have wild swings in profitability, particularly if those swings are clearly tied to market conditions.** The mortgage industry is a good example because it is impacted significantly by interest rates, which cannot be controlled by the organization.

In any situation, it's a good idea to write a caveat into your plan that allows for management to adjust the payout if something outside of normal operations creates an inordinately high payout situation. Other examples include the sale of a significant asset or unexpected income from investments.

If you do decide to cap your plan for one of the reasons I've stated, the final question is "what should the cap be?" There is no formula, and I suggest that the number you choose will ensure that the short- and long-term goals of the company will be met.

If you have a nonprofit or some other organizational structure where you have any doubts about the legality of your plan, it is always wise to consult a lawyer who has some expertise in that area. In most metropolitan areas, you can contact an employer assistance organization as a resource (in Denver, for example, there is an organization called the Mountain States Employers Council).

DISTRIBUTION METHOD

This is often the biggest discussion point of an incentive plan. Now that we have identified the pool of money that might be available to employees, how will it be distributed to them? I will offer three alternatives, and one of them will fit the needs or situations of most organizations.

The first distribution method, and perhaps the most common, is distribution based on wages. In other words, the individual employee's compensation divided by the total wages of the company will determine the payout for that individual. With this method, every employee receives an incentive payout that is the same percentage of his or her salary. Given this, employees with higher salaries will receive larger incentives (in terms of dollars). Most employees will accept this as an equitable method of distribution, understanding that people with higher salaries have more responsibility, more experience, and are typically salaried rather than hourly and therefore exempt from overtime pay.

The second method is simply equal distribution of the incentive pool among all employees, regardless of their positions or compensation (see Table 2.2). This is very easy to administer—the incentive pool is divided by the number of employees and distributed accordingly. It also sends a very powerful message (we're all in this together), which is perhaps why the companies that use this method statistically (from my experience) perform better. I should point out that this statistic is not entirely reliable, however, due to the fact that the majority of companies that share incentives equally are smaller and flatter (meaning, companies that have fewer levels of management). The larger and more complex a company is, the less likely it is to choose this method.

The final method of distribution to discuss is distribution based on shares. I am not referring to equity here but rather attaching a number of shares to different levels in the organization, typically based on responsibility and impact on organizational performance. For example, administrative and field personnel may receive one share, mid-level management may receive two, and senior leadership may receive three (these are only examples). With this method, the distribution of incentive dollars will be based on the number of shares assigned to the employee given his or her position in the organization. Although I am not particularly keen on this method, as it resembles a "caste" system (at least that is how it can be perceived), it does make sense in some industries. The construction industry and other related industries, for example, often adopt this model because some organization members (such as project managers) can have a very significant impact on the profitability of the organization and therefore should (perhaps) have a greater incentive opportunity. Generally speaking, however, distributing an incentive based on wages accomplishes much the same thing, but without the perception of inequity.

SHOULD THE PLAN BE QUARTERLY, ANNUAL, OR SOMETHING ELSE?

The most effective way to shape behavior is by rewarding it quickly. For this reason, I suggest quarterly payout opportunities for most companies as opposed to annual ones (monthly payouts are typically too difficult to administer, but might be even better if feasible). Some companies have gotten into trouble with quarterly incentive plans because they do not think their plans through, and therefore they calculate the incentive payouts the same way every quarter. For example, what would happen if a company had two strong quarters (and therefore large incentive payouts) at the beginning of the year and then tanked the last two quarters? I suppose it could ask its employees to return their incentive checks (although that is unlikely to work and may in fact be illegal). Given the potential of this situation, we suggest that the company withhold 50 percent of the payouts for each of the first three quarters and make an adjustment at year-end based on how the company finishes up the year. With this method, and given that the company does not tank, employees receive roughly one-eighth of their incentive pay in each of the first three quarters and five-eighths in the last quarter. This allows for a quarterly incentive opportunity while still protecting the cash flow of the company in the event of a downturn.

SEPARATE MANAGEMENT POOLS

I have encountered many business owners who feel strongly about providing larger incentive opportunities for leadership, particularly if this is something they have done historically, and/or is common in their industry. In such cases, I will typically acquiesce and design a separate plan for the leadership team. Generally, the design is the same as the broad-based plan (with a significantly smaller percentage of PBT paid into the plan), and people in this group will participate in both plans. One suggestion: if you have a separate leadership pool, I suggest you communicate this to your nonmanagement employees. If you do not, they will find out anyway, and you may then have a morale issue to deal with. You may communicate to them that this is one of the reasons to aspire to leadership.

I have some final comments on the incentive plan designs I'm suggesting, which are all based on organizational performance rather than individual performance. A question that invariably comes up when I am discussing incentive plans with a client is "what about the superstars?" In other words, it doesn't seem fair that a slouch would be receiving the same incentive opportunity as a superstar performer. *This is not an incentive issue; it is a management issue.* In other words, why are you hanging on to the slouch? As I've mentioned before, what most companies do is hire quickly and fire slowly, which is always a bad management strategy, but particularly so in a company practicing Ownership Thinking. If someone does not fit, make that determination and take action. Remember that if you delay making the difficult decision of terminating someone, it not only hurts the company, but also damages your credibility as a leader. When a poor performer is finally terminated, the surrounding employees are thinking "what took them so long?"

Also, remember that you want to see *organizations* of excellence, not simply *pockets* of excellence in an organization. When an incentive plan is tied to organizational performance, and an environment of high visibility is created at the same time, employees become far less tolerant of poor performance. They will typically help an employee with questionable performance either rise to the occasion or find the door. It creates a self-selecting environment.

Finally, there are other ways to reward superstars. These would include salary increases, recognition, and growth opportunities, to name a few.

Stock Appreciation Rights

Stock Appreciation Rights (SARs) are a form of synthetic equity (in other words, not actual stock) that provides the grantee with the appreciation, if any, in the value of the underlying stock from the date of grant to the date of exercise. I am including a section on SARs in this book, and specifically in this chapter, for three reasons:

First, SARs are simply another form of cash incentive and so do not necessarily belong in a discussion of stock plans. The most significant difference between a SARs plan and an incentive plan tied to PBT (as discussed in this chapter) is that SARs are tied to the stock value of the organization.

Second, SARs (and other forms of synthetic equity, such as Phantom Stock plans) offer an opportunity to provide to employees (typically only leadership, but not in all cases) cash incentive opportunities that are tied to value, not just to profit. Stock value may be affected by profit, but there are several other influencers—

many of which are tied to balance sheet considerations—such as asset value, return on assets, and cash flow. Given this, it is an opportunity to focus recipients of such plans on the balance sheet and value without providing actual stock ownership (which some business owners may not be willing to do).

Third, incentive plans as described in this chapter may entice employees to stay on until the end of a fiscal year (given the hold-back), but beyond that the plans are not much of a retention tool. SARs typically vest over several years and may also be distributed over a period of time beyond the vesting period; therefore they can be a tool to retain valued staff members.

A SARs program typically includes the following features:

- Participants do not make a capital investment in the company but instead have a contractual right to receive a future payment from the company pending satisfaction of the terms and conditions of the program.

- Participants are rewarded based only on the excess, if any, of the value of the company from time of grant to time of exercise. For example, if one share of stock has increased in value from $50 to $60, then the SAR value is $10.

- Participants can exercise and realize the value of their SARs at their election (once vesting has occurred) or upon occurrence of a specified triggering event. Triggering events include the following:

  - Sale of company

- Public offering

- Death or disability

- Retirement

- Resignation

■ In the case of the first three triggering events noted above, SARs will typically vest immediately, and they may be exercised immediately.

■ Participants will typically forfeit their SARs if they are terminated for any grievous circumstances, such as fraud, theft, or starting a competing business.

■ When SARs awards are settled, they are treated in the same way as deferred cash compensation. The recipient of the award pays taxes on the award at such time as it is received, and it is taxed as ordinary income. If the recipient wishes to defer the receipt of the payout, he or she must make this declaration 12 months prior to vesting.

Table 2.3 is an example of a SARs schedule for an executive in a $25 million engineering firm.

The executive in this plan was awarded 4,000 SARs, which vested in equal increments over a period of five years, beginning in 2004. In addition to the five-year vesting period, there was a three-year payout period for awards earned in any given year. So

TABLE 2.3 Payouts

Year	Vested	Value	Vested Value	2004	2005	2006	2007	2008	2009	2010	Total
2003	0	$126	$0	$0	$0	$0	$0	$0	$0	$0	
2004	800	$140	$11,200	$3,733	$3,733	$3,733					
2005	1,600	$155	$35,200		$11,733	$11,733	$11,733				
2006	2,400	$150	$11,200			$3,733	$3,733	$3,733			
2007	3,200	$170	$83,200				$27,733	$27,733	$27,733		
2008	4,000	$190	$115,200					$38,400	$38,400	$38,400	
			Totals	$3,733	$15,467	$19,200	$43,200	$69,867	$66,133	$38,400	$256,000

the total payout period, as you see in the table, was seven years. The total value of the SARs awards is noted in the lower right hand corner of the spreadsheet ($256,000).

The Argument Against Incentive Plans

In his excellent book, *Drive*, Daniel Pink makes a compelling argument against the use of if, then incentives. He professes that cash incentives may have been effective motivators in the twentieth century, but may, in fact, create the wrong behavioral results in today's organizations. In the book, he states that "Rewards can perform a weird sort of behavioral alchemy: They can transform an interesting task into a drudge. They can turn play into work." He goes on to note what he calls "The Seven Deadly Flaws" of incentive plans:

1. They can extinguish intrinsic motivation.

2. They can diminish performance.

3. They can crush creativity.

4. They can crowd out good behavior.

5. They can encourage cheating, shortcuts, and unethical behavior.

6. They can become addictive.

7. They can foster short-term thinking.

What motivates employees in today's workplace, he says, are autonomy, mastery, and purpose. I agree with this premise, and I share his concerns about *most* incentive plans, which do not incorporate the cultural and educational elements outlined in this book. Pink does indeed make a compelling argument against incentives, and therefore I believe it's important to point out the reasons that his argument does not apply to incentive plans in an Ownership Thinking environment. To do this, I will address below each of the "flaws" noted in his book.

1. **They can extinguish intrinsic motivation.** In an Ownership Thinking culture, incentive rewards, or pay-outs, *are in fact intrinsic rewards.* In a recent Super Group meeting (The Super Group is an invitation-only group of extraordinary CEOs that meets three times a year to discuss best practices), my member CEOs and I had a discussion around this. Though all of these CEOs had had their share of challenges around incentives in the past, it was universally agreed that incentive plans in an Ownership Thinking culture were indeed very effective. In these environments, the incentive rewards are appreciated for their monetary value; however, the real incentive for employees is knowing that they've won and being able to see their contributions toward that win.

2. **They can diminish performance.** This does not occur in the high-visibility, high-engagement environment created by practicing Ownership Thinking. Performance is not only gauged by financial rewards, but by all of the

73

learning and excitement associated with "playing the game."

3. **They can crush creativity.** There are a myriad of ways to express individual and team creativity in an Ownership Thinking culture, most notably with Rapid Improvement Plans.

4. **They can crowd out good behavior.** Unlikely in the high-visibility environment created with Ownership Thinking.

5. **They can encourage cheating, shortcuts, and unethical behavior.** Again, unlikely in the high-visibility environment created with Ownership Thinking.

6. **They can become addictive.** Yes, they can. However the addiction in an Ownership Thinking environment is not an addiction to money or to entitlement or to security, but rather to winning.

7. **They can foster short-term thinking.** There is some potential of this happening in an Ownership Thinking culture. To combat short-term thinking, it is important for leadership to communicate clearly and consistently the importance of decisions on both short- and long-term performance and to provide specific opportunities for employees, whenever possible, to learn this lesson. For example, if an acquisition is to be made that will put

the company in a better long-term competitive position in the marketplace, it may have a short-term negative impact on the company's financial performance and, therefore, on incentive payout opportunities. Employees should be provided information as to why the decision was made and what the long-term benefits are to the organization and to their future in it.

KEY CONCEPTS

■ Incentive plans must be self-funded.

■ Most incentive plans don't work. In fact, many of them actually damage the organization. There are three reasons for this:

• They are too complicated.

• They are tied to financial performance, but no effort is made to teach employees about finance.

• There is no connection between the work the employees are doing and the incentive payouts they receive (or don't receive).

■ Due to the above noted points, most incentives are simply entitlements.

■ Incentives should be tied to organizational performance rather than to individual or departmental performance.

■ Incentive plans should be simple in design and generally tied to one key indicator: profit before tax.

■ SARs are another form of cash incentive. They are tied to stock value rather than to profitability and are useful retention tools.

■ The arguments made against incentive plans are not valid in an Ownership Thinking culture.

CHAPTER THREE

Your Employees Think You Make Wheelbarrows of Money

n this chapter, I will provide some tools to assist you in teaching your employees about business and finance. But first, let's look at why educating your employees is so important.

The primary reason for providing business acumen training to employees (and for sharing more information than you might be accustomed to) is this: *What your employees don't know can hurt the company.* I'll give you one example from literally hundreds I have seen to illustrate my point. I was working with a corrugated box manufacturer in 2008 and had already done all of the leadership work—identified the KPIs, built the scoreboard, designed the incentive plan, and so on—and was then working on the employee training. My company utilizes a program that we designed over the years that we call Money Matters. For the first training session, I had about 35 employees, primarily from the shop floor. The leadership in this organization had never shared financial information with its employees before, so this was totally new for them. I started the session with the following question: "Your company had $12 million in sales last year. What do you think the profit was?" One of the employees raised his hand, shrugged his shoulders, and said: "50 percent."

I suspect many of you know that that percentage is highly unlikely. In my experience with hundreds of companies, I have never come across one with a 50 percent profit (I'd probably be in that business if I did!). In fact, 5 to 10 percent is closer to the norm. Here is something to consider: *In the absence of information, people make stuff up.* When I ask this question of employees in companies where financial information has not been shared (or business acumen taught), 50 percent is a pretty common answer (I encourage you to ask your employees this question—it's quite an eye opener). Sometimes I hear 100 percent, if you can imagine. As silly as that may sound, many people associate revenues with profits. Here was the reality in this corrugated box company—in 2007, the company broke even (meaning it made no profit). And in the four years prior to that, it had averaged a 1.5 percent profit. This is a low margin industry, *but not that low*. Why, then, do you think it might be a problem that the company's employees believed that the company was making a 50 percent profit? There are two primary problems here.

The first problem is that when employees assume their company is making wheelbarrows of money, they become wasteful. In fact, there's almost a bitterness going on in the back of their minds. The thought process is something like this: "So what that we scrapped that run (or wasted that labor or damaged that product or shipped the wrong order or had to return to a job and perform some rework). We're rolling in the dough." And, by the way, they don't say, *"We're* rolling in the dough." They say, *"He* (or *she) is* rolling in the dough," pointing of course to the owner. This leads to the second problem: when employees believe the company (or owner) is making so much money, the obvious next question is: "Where's my piece of that huge profit?" As you might imagine, this can create a morale problem.

There is a tremendous irony in all of this, as well. The primary fear that business owners have about sharing financial information with employees is this: "If I do disclose the company's finances and my employees know how much money the company is making, they're all going to want more." What those owners don't know is that the employees currently think the company is making a 50 percent profit! The truth is, employees are typically shocked when they see the real cost of doing business. In fact, they are often disbelieving at first, until they have been exposed to the numbers long enough to see the truth in them.

The other fear I generally hear from business owners about teaching finance and sharing information with employees is: "What if our competitors get their hands on the information?" Although there may be some legitimacy to this concern, consider what a competitor would do with that information. They are in the same industry. They deal with the same kind of issues you deal with (suppliers, marketplace, etc.). Do you really think there would be any big surprises here? Therefore, I do think that we should share the amount of information that employees need to know to do the very best job they can. However, certain information, for example rebates from suppliers, could hurt the company if it were divulged and, therefore, *it should not be shared*. That is why I seldom use the term *open-book management* or promote the idea of full disclosure of information to all employees.

Now that you know the importance of teaching your employees about business and finance and engaging them more in the organization's financial performance, the next question is: how do you effectively teach them?

Over the years, I have learned that associating personal finance with business finance is the most effective way to teach finance to nonfinancial employees. Why? First of all, this takes the intimidation out of a potentially intimidating subject. Most people assume that finance is very complex, when in fact it really is not (like anything, we can make it complex). Second, personal and business finance are very much the same.

My company uses a lot of graphics and examples in our training program. When looking at Income Statements, Cash Flow Statements, and Balance Sheets, we include pictures of cameras on our slides to make our point. Income Statements and Cash Flow Statements are represented by a picture of a video camera graphic, meaning they are dynamic, or moving. The Balance Sheet, on the other hand, is more like a snapshot of your organization's health at a given moment in time and, therefore, is represented with a more traditional SLR.

So, we take a picture of the organization's health (the Balance Sheet), and then we work with the employees to examine a period of time when lots of activity occurred (say a month). Sales were made, expenses were incurred (Income Statement), cash came in, and cash went out (Cash Flow Statement). At the end of that time frame, we take another picture. Obviously, we hope that the financial picture had improved.

These three financial statements (Cash Flow Statement, Income Statement, and Balance Sheet) are actually quite simple to understand and communicate. Each statement has three core components. Your best method for showing these to your employees is to begin by breaking down each into these components.

The Income Statement tends to be the financial statement that is emphasized the most in organizations. The three primary components of an Income Statement are *sales* (or revenue), less *expenses*, which equals *Profit Before Tax* (*PBT*). When teaching employees (or management, for that matter) about Income Statements, this is where I like to start. Also, it is important that they understand the effect of taxes and that roughly 40 percent of that PBT will go to Uncle Sam (employees are generally shocked to hear this, as well). So, that is an Income Statement. It is simple, even though, most likely, it will be a few pages long because of a variety of entries in the broad categories of revenue and expenses.

The Cash Flow Statement is an entirely different animal, and it is important that your employees understand the differences because they will be expected to help to improve both statements. When I teach people about the Cash Flow Statement, I start with this simple question: "What happens to cash in your household?" Most people will say something like, "It disappears!" or, "My wife (or husband, or kid) spends it!" In other words, it goes out. But cash also comes in. So, cash comes into your household and it goes out of your household, and what's left over is your change in cash. The same thing applies in business: cash comes in (collections, loans, sale of assets) and cash goes out (expense payments, loan payments, capital expenditures), and what's left over is its change in cash.

So what exactly is the difference between the Income Statement and the Cash Flow Statement? The primary difference (in most industries) is timing. When a product or service is sold to a customer, the customer typically has a specified time period to pay for it. This is called the *term of payment*. Thirty days to pay is a typical term of payment; however, the average number of days an organization takes to collect is rarely the same as its term. Customers like to hold on to their money as long as they can. If there are any problems with the transaction and delivery of product or service, this can delay payment. Perhaps there is an error on the invoice or purchase order, the shipment is partial, the wrong product is shipped, or there is a quality issue with the product or service. Can employees help to improve collections? Of course they can, assuming we teach them how. Remember that when your customers have your cash, *you don't have it.*

It is also very important to teach your employees why the company needs cash. When employees are asked what the company uses the cash for, the first thing they will typically say is payroll. Payroll is the largest expense in most organizations, but there are many other expenses: equipment operation, fuel, materials, facilities, utilities, telecommunications, and travel and entertainment, to name just a few. In addition, if an organization wants to remain competitive and grow, it needs cash for things beyond expenses found on the Income Statement. These would include equipment purchases, capital improvements, debt retirement, and retained earnings; items that we find on our third and final financial statement, the balance sheet.

The contents of a Balance Sheet can be viewed in its easiest form as including what the organization owns, what it owes, and what it *really* owns. When I teach employees about Balance Sheets, I like to use the example of a house. I may ask for a show of hands from people who own houses. My next question is, "Do you really own that house?" All or most people will not own their houses and will instead have mortgages, so you might say that the bank owns a certain percentage of their houses (often the largest percentage). The third component, what they really own, is simply the equity they have in their houses. (When I address my audiences, I typically say "the two windows that you really own," which generally gets laughs).

This analogy can now be applied to business. As opposed to the house, a business *owns* things like equipment, buildings,

83

inventory, and accounts receivables. It *owes* both short- (Accounts Payables) and long-term debt. It *really owns* things like equity and retained earnings. Figure 3.1 is an excellent (albeit somewhat messy) graphic of the three financial statements and how they fit together.

In Chapter 2, I suggest that incentives generally be tied to the organization's PBT. If you do this in your business, it's obviously very important to teach your employees about finance and to engage them in finding the money to fund the incentive. You should also teach them about capital expenditures (purchases of equipment, for example) and how they affect the incentive plan. As I mentioned earlier, in the absence of information, people make stuff up (that is, they make assumptions). Using capital expenditures as an example, imagine that your company has an incentive

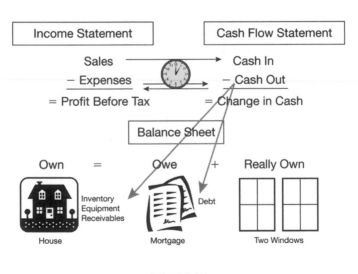

FIGURE 3.1

plan tied to PBT and that you have not taught anyone how finance works. The company spends $100k on a new piece of equipment. How do you think your employees are going to feel about that expenditure? Well, they're probably not going to be too excited about it. Why? Because, most likely, their assumption (logical, but incorrect) will be that the $100k was an expense, thus lowering the company's PBT by that amount and cutting into their incentive plan. Of course, this is not true. Here's how it really works. Let's say the company has $50k in cash to spend on that same equipment. It borrows the remaining $50k and now has a $100k piece of equipment on the Balance Sheet—something it owns. There was no effect on the Income Statement or on the incentive plan. *Not in the first month.* In subsequent months, there are a few new expenses, however. The first expense I typically associate with buying a new car. You buy a car, drive it off the lot, and drive it around for a few months. What happens to it? It depreciates. The same thing applies to equipment. The depreciation is not one lump sum, however. It is chunked into monthly amounts over the lifetime of that equipment (the government dictates this schedule). The second expense would be interest. The company in our example borrowed some money to purchase the equipment, so it also has an interest expense every month until the equipment is paid off. The third and final expense may be some maintenance or other costs associated with the equipment. But, because the equipment was purchased to increase revenue or improve efficiency, assuming it was in fact utilized efficiently, it should make the company more than enough money to offset these new expenses. This is important to tell employees because you want them to feel good about growth—assuming it is smart growth.

I mentioned earlier that my company has created a financial acumen training program to teach employees the fundamentals of business and finance and to help them to engage in the organization's financial performance (see our Web site for details). On the following pages, you'll find some examples and exercises from that program that you may put to use in your business.

This first exercise is a lot of fun and quite an eye opener for both employees and ownership. Set up the exercise like this:

- Imagine that you have a company that generates a 5 percent profit on average. If you were to sell a dollar's worth of product or service, how much of that would end up on the profit line? Of course, the answer is a nickel.

- What if you were to save a dollar (or $10,000)? This may be the result of reducing rework or scrap, improving labor efficiencies or reducing overtime, or reducing set-up time on equipment. There are a myriad of ways one might save money. Every time you save a dollar in your business, the entire dollar goes to the bottom line.

- Now, let's emphasize the importance of this. In the example above, if you were to save a dollar (or $10,000), which, again, will go directly to the profit line, how much revenue will it take to get that money to the profit line? The answer is 20 times that amount (if you have a 5 percent profit, as noted previously). This is rather simplistic and could be debated, but it makes a great point and most employees will not challenge it.

86

■   Here is a more tangible example. A recent client in the office furniture distribution business was running at about $10 million in annual sales and averaging roughly 3 percent PBT (which was about par with the industry standard). One of the company's key issues was errors, which in that industry consists of things like finish, fabric, pricing, and damage. This one area was costing the company about $160k per year. If it were to reduce this error rate by 75 percent (which it did with a Rapid Improvement Plan—discussed in Chapter 5), it would mean a cost savings of $120k, all of which would fall to the bottom line. Consider this: how much revenue would it take at a 3 percent profit margin to bring $120k to the bottom line? The answer is $4 million ($120k divided by 3 percent). *And this is only one key indicator!* Just imagine what might be accomplished by focusing on 8 or 10 or 12 key indicators that all have the same level of effect on the company.

Now, here is the exercise:

■   Have your employees form small groups of about five employees in each group.

■   Take out a short stack of dollar bills and tell the group: "Imagine that this is our revenue and that this table in front of me is our business. As we go through the month, we are spending this money on all of our expenses, such as payroll, materials cost, facilities, fleet, and so on (lay the bills down on the table a few at a time as you say this, and finish with one bill left in your hand). What's left over here is our profit (waving the bill). Now, the majority of this money went toward our expenses. But there are a bunch of cracks in this table, and a lot of this money is simply falling through the cracks. The cracks are two things. The first bunch of cracks is our inefficiencies—things like scrap, rework, unbilled time, and downtime. Having said that, I've never seen a company become truly best in class by focusing all of its attention on cost controls. It's also about taking advantage of opportunities, like new product development, new market opportunities, better technologies, or acquisitions. If an opportunity presents itself, and we don't take advantage of it, then this is a crack as well."

- Give your employees about 10 minutes or so to brainstorm and list the "cracks in the company's table." Where are those inefficiencies and missed opportunities in the company? At the end of that time, go around the room a few times and ask each group to read one item from their list each time around. Write the items mentioned on a flip chart.

- When the page is full, stop and ask employees participating in the exercise: "How much money do you think is on this piece of paper?" Lead them a little bit by asking: "Do you think there is a hundred thousand dollars here? Two hundred? Three?" Stop when they want to stop. I recently did this with a $16-million optics company, and they stopped at $500k. And they were right—there was easily $500k on that piece of paper. I then took a calculator and said: "OK, you think you found $500k? Let's divide that number by your profit percent for last year, which was 6 percent, to see what you'd have to sell to get that much money to the bottom line. Wow! You would have to sell an additional $8.3 million in order to get this money you just found!"

There are two primary points to this exercise. The first is that there is nothing magical about business. The money is real, and it's there for the finding. Second, it should help employees to begin feeling more confident about their ability to find the money that will, in part, be funding their incentive plan.

The exercise is meant to get employees thinking about both inefficiencies and missed opportunities. My experience is that most groups will focus primarily on inefficiencies in this exercise because inefficiencies are so visible and are what you might call the "low-hanging fruit." Here is another exercise to get your employees focused entirely on opportunities and innovation:

- Keep your employees in the same groups as they were during the previous exercise.

- Start by pointing out that the list on the flip chart from the previous exercise is primarily focused on inefficiencies and waste—the low-hanging fruit. Tell them that now they are going to do another exercise focused entirely on process improvements and innovations.

■ For this exercise, ask the participants to start by putting on an (imaginary) entrepreneur hat. Then ask them how entrepreneurs think and act that makes them different from other people. Generally, you'll hear comments similar to these:

- They take risks.

- They think outside the box.

- If they fail at something, they get up and try again.

- They don't accept the status quo.

■ Now ask them to brainstorm once again, but this time focusing on ideas for improvement in the organization or ideas that are totally innovative.

■ After another 10 minutes or so, go around the room once again and write their thoughts on your flip chart. Again, ask how much money is on this piece of paper.

A final thought on these exercises: The cracks in the company that the employees came up with in the first exercise (cracks in the table) are generally the low-hanging fruit, and, therefore, it is fairly easy to make improvements in a short period of time and with minimal (if any) investment. However, the items from the second exercise generally require more thought and often some investment of time and/or capital. Another way to express this is that items from the first exercise are tactical, while items from the second are strategic.

Both exercises work wonderfully in virtually any business environment. Any additional exercises we do in our financial acumen training sessions are tailored to the organization and focused on the company's specific issues. Examples include:

■ Average collection days (Accounts Receivable)

■ Inventory turns

■ Billable time

■ Scrap or rework

■ Equipment utilization and/or set-up time

■ Pricing

For example, what follows is an exercise focused on average collection days (the average number of days it takes to collect from customers) and the effect this has on the organization. This example is from a construction company that does about $50 million a year in revenue. The exercise can be done in small groups, and employees can then report their ideas and insights.

SCENARIO

- Average collection days at our company are running around 50 (meaning customers pay us an average of 50 days after we have invoiced them).

QUESTIONS FOR CONSIDERATION

- How do average collection days affect our Income Statement?

- How do they affect our Cash Flow Statement?

- What departments have an effect on average collection days?

    1.

    2.

    3.

    4.

- If average collection days could be reduced from 50 to 40, approximately how much cash would this bring into the business?

Monthly Sales	$4,200,000
Divided by Days in Month	30
Equals Daily Potential Collections	$
X 10 (50 – 40)	$

- What could this cash be used for? Could this affect the Income Statement?

- What actions can be taken to improve this situation?

Typically I would give employees about 15 minutes to work on this exercise. Once they are done, turn their attention to the front of the room (with you) and review the answers. The discussion will generally revolve around the following thoughts:

- At first glance, it does not seem that average collection days affect the income statement. Revenues would remain the same, as this is based on what is invoiced, not what is received. But what about expenses? These may be affected in a couple of different ways. If we are not collecting regularly, we still of course must pay our bills and the company may have to borrow money to do this. If the company must borrow money, it will have an interest expense. In addition, suppliers will often offer discounts for early payment. If the company does not have cash on hand due to slow collections, it may not be able to capitalize on those discounts.

- Average collection days will obviously affect the Cash Flow Statement directly. Every dollar not received will reduce our cash flow by that amount.

- One of the most important outcomes of this exercise is that employees can see that virtually every department has an effect on average collection days. Some examples are as follows:

- The salesperson did not relay the terms of payment clearly when making the sale and/or it is not clear in the contract.

- There were inaccuracies in the invoice, or perhaps the invoice was sent to the wrong person.

- The product or service was not satisfactory to the customer; there were quality issues.

- It was a partial shipment of product, or a service was not completed on time.

■ To determine the amount of cash brought into the business by reducing average collection days by 10, monthly sales are divided by the number of days in the month to determine how much would be collected each day if collections were made daily and in equal installments ($4,200,000/30 = $140,000). This is then multiplied by the reduction in collection days, which is 10. So, the answer to the question is $1,400,000 ($140,000 × 10). The cash could be used to retire debt, take discounts from suppliers, purchase new equipment, and so on. All of these would affect the Income Statement.

- A variety of things could be done to improve the situation, most of which would be in alignment with how different departments affect collections, as noted in our earlier discussion.

Advanced Financial Acumen

When teaching finance to employees, don't assume that your management team members are particularly savvy in this area. I have worked with hundreds of management teams, and it's clear to me that many people in management roles are not particularly well educated in the area of finance. This is not a criticism. If someone focuses on marketing in his or her education and career and becomes a VP of marketing, this does not make that person a wizard in finance. The same applies to HR, sales, operations, or any other nonfinancial function. In fact, I've come across more than a few small business owners who were not that financially literate but who might have been experts in the technical aspects of their industries and created businesses based on their technical expertise. I've also learned that often people in leadership or ownership roles are not comfortable acknowledging their lack of financial acumen because they are a bit embarrassed about it. Given this, they should participate in the financial acumen training along with nonmanagement employees. To help your management (and perhaps yourself) save face, simply let it be known that everyone is participating in the training, which sends a message of solidarity. Keep in mind that whatever roles people play in an organization, and at whatever level, they are apt to make better

95

decisions in those roles if they have an understanding of the financial ramifications of their decisions.

Although what I've outlined so far in this chapter is relatively basic, it is important to train your employees in this fashion, even people in leadership roles who have had some finance education. In addition to training literally thousands of employees over the years, both management and nonmanagement, I have also taught business and finance at both the undergraduate and graduate levels in college. I mention this because I have yet to come across any textbooks that teach finance in a fashion similar to the approach I've outlined in this chapter. It's a pity because many of the students I've encountered in those college programs did not really have a strong foundation on the subject and seemed to be at least a bit lost in it all. Given this, whenever I teach classes, at whatever level, I always include material similar to what I'm presenting here, which has been universally appreciated.

Table 3.1 is an absolutely fantastic mechanism for teaching people about financial statements at a somewhat higher level of sophistication—financial acumen 201, I suppose. I've come across this model here and there over the years, and generally use it when I'm training leadership teams in finance. Not only is it a great training tool, it's also a fantastic way to get all of your financial statements together in one place for executive meetings or board meetings. I believe this approach can be attributed to Lou Mobley, who created and directed IBM's Executive School. The beauty of it goes beyond merely seeing them side by side; it is structured in a way that actually shows the relationships among the three financial statements and also makes clear certain concepts that people often struggle with, such as how a company can be profit-

TABLE 3.1

Beginning Balance Sheet		Income Statement		Cash Flow Statement		Ending Balance Sheet	
Cash	$50,000			Change in Cash	($7,000)	Cash	$43,000
AR	$180,000	Revenue	$210,000	Collections	$200,000	AR	$190,000
Inventory	$200,000	Cost of Materials	$65,000	Materials Payments	$70,000	Inventory	$205,000
		Direct Labor	$55,000	Direct Labor Payments	$55,000		
Fixed Assets	$220,000	Depreciation	$5,000			Fixed Assets	$215,000
Total Assets	$650,000					Total Assets	$653,000
		Total S, G, & A Expenses	$58,000	S, G, & A Expense Payments	$62,000		
AP	$180,000	Income Tax	$7,000	Tax Payments	$10,000	AP	$176,000
Taxes Due	$3,000					Taxes Due	$0
Long-Term Debt	$65,000					Long-Term Debt	$65,000
Total Liabilities	$248,000					Total Liabilities	$241,000
Retained Earnings	$402,000	Net Profit	$20,000	Dividends	$10,000	Retained Earnings	$412,000
Total Equity	$402,000					Total Equity	$412,000
Liabilities + Equity	$650,000					Liabilities + Equity	$653,000

able (Income Statement) and yet have a negative cash flow (Cash Flow Statement). In this model, the company is profitable (Income Statement) yet has a negative cash flow (Cash Flow Statement). This is true because Accounts Receivables and Inventory have both grown, which may highlight a problem in effectively managing these areas. If you are using this format in Excel, you can also play "what if" by making changes in some areas to see the effect in others.

Here are some additional examples of what you can learn from this model:

- Beginning Cash (on the Beginning Balance Sheet), plus Change in Cash (Cash Flow Statement), equals your Ending Cash (Ending Balance Sheet). Note that the Change in Cash is negative, so the ending cash balance is less than the beginning cash balance.

- Beginning AR (Accounts Receivables, on the Beginning Balance Sheet), plus revenue (Income Statement), minus collections (Cash Flow Statement), equals your Ending Accounts Receivables.

- Beginning Inventory (Beginning Balance Sheet), plus Cost of Materials (Income Statement), minus Materials Payments (Cash Flow Statement), equals Ending Inventory (Ending Balance Sheet).

- Fixed Assets (Beginning Balance Sheet), minus Depreciation (Income Statement), equals Fixed Assets (Ending Balance Sheet). Note that this is not addressed on the Cash Flow Statement, because it is a noncash event.

- AP (Accounts Payables) is treated the same as Accounts Receivables, as are Taxes.

- Retained Earnings (Beginning Balance Sheet), plus Net Profit (Income Statement), minus Dividends (Cash Flow Statement), equals Ending Retained Earnings.

A few final notes on financial acumen training for employees. A variety of good programs exist (ours being one of them, of course) for teaching finance. I suggest you poke around until you find something that you like and, most important, seems intuitive to you. If you decide to develop a program internally and have a staff person from your company teach it, then your CFO or controller would be a logical choice. If it is your CFO (or controller) who will be teaching the program, make sure to communicate to them that the purpose of financial training in this case is to help nonfinancial people gain an understanding of finance in a manner that is (1) not intimidating to them and (2) useful to them in their decision making (both in the business and at home, you might add). This is important to point out, because I've seen programs designed and delivered by finance executives that were either way over the heads of the trainees or excruciatingly boring, or both. Finance executives should not use this exercise to show everyone just how brilliant and well educated they are or to protect their jobs by hinting that no one else can do them. Furthermore, more often than not, the resulting improved financial acumen of employees will ultimately make the CFO's job much easier, since employees will be able to make better decisions that improve financial performance and make financial reporting more timely and accurate.

KEY CONCEPTS

- In the absence of information, people make stuff up.

- Most employees believe their companies are far more profitable than they actually are, and they become wasteful because of this belief.

- When teaching finance to nonfinancial employees, associate personal finance with business finance to take the intimidation out of finance and to make it more relevant.

- Finance is not terribly complex.

- There is a difference between profit and cash. In fact, a company can be profitable and run out of cash. Employees should be engaged not only in driving profitability, but in generating cash.

- Use exercises in a workshop setting to engage employees in learning about finance and identifying solutions to organizational inefficiencies or missed opportunities.

- Don't assume that your leadership team is financially savvy. Include them in financial training.

- If your CFO or Controller will be teaching finance to employees, make sure that they do so in a manner that employees can understand and utilize.

CHAPTER FOUR

Measure Through the Windshield, Not the Rearview Mirror

This chapter focuses primarily on Key Performance Indicators, or KPIs, which I define as "the *operational* and financial measures that will have the greatest impact on the success (or failure) of your company." The word *operational* is italicized here because operational measures are the activity-based, leading measures that actually drive financial performance and are more important in this regard than lagging, financial measures. Interestingly, these leading measures are not an area of focus in many organizations and may not even be identified. In this chapter, then, I will explore the following:

- Why using only financial statements to "keep score" is not enough, particularly if you want to engage your employees

- Some examples of KPIs from different organizations and industries

- How to identify your organization's KPIs

- How to build effective scoreboards

- How to have effective forecasting sessions

Remember that Ownership Thinking is about engaging *all* of your employees in the financial performance of the company, not just leadership. Simply identifying your KPIs and monitoring them at the senior level will not necessarily drive performance. It is critical to use scoreboards in a high-involvement fashion and to engage all employees in improving specific KPIs through the use of Rapid Improvement Plans (Chapter 5). "Share the insomnia," a phrase we like to use at Ownership Thinking, means that every employee in your organization should be focused on the same issues. Why should you as the business owner or leader be the only one losing sleep?

Why Financial Statements Are Not Enough

As I mentioned in the Introduction, companies traditionally "keep score" with financial statements: Income Statements, Cash Flow Statements, and Balance Sheets. Keeping in mind that Ownership Thinking is largely about engaging employees in the financial performance of the company, logically speaking, you will have to begin sharing some financial information with your employees. This does not mean that you must share detailed financial statements with them, however. In fact, there are several reasons why using financial statements to keep score with employees might not be adequate:

1. Financial statements are historical documents. By the time they are available, it is too late to do anything about the results. Given this, organizations tend to manage their businesses somewhat reactively. It's as if they were managing through the rearview mirror.

2. Most employees never see detailed financial statements. But even if they did (and again, I'm not suggesting that they must), they probably wouldn't understand them nor could they use them to make decisions. In fact, as noted in the previous chapter, many people on management teams are not particularly savvy when it comes to reading financials.

3. Financial statements tell you nothing more than the score at the end of the game. They tell you nothing about what occurred during the game that got you to that score.

4. Many business owners and/or leaders are uncomfortable with the idea of sharing detailed financial information with employees.

Before moving on, I need to address number 4 above—the discomfort that some business owners and/or leaders have with sharing financial information with employees. These concerns were addressed (and hopefully debunked) in the previous chapter, but I want to emphasize that there is a difference between Ownership Thinking and something called *Open-Book Management* (*OBM*). OBM is a term (and philosophy, I suppose) that has been around for many years and generally suggests full disclosure of financial information to all employees (typically with the exception of salaries). I generally don't use this term or push this agenda. Aside from the fear factors noted previously, there are three other reasons for this:

- I don't believe that full disclosure is necessary. Rather, I believe that employees simply need to receive the information necessary for them to do the best job they can.

- Employees do better when they are focused not on detailed financials but rather on leading, activity-based measures that are driving financial results. The actual financial results may be shown in a very simplified manner (more about this later in our discussion of scoreboards).

- I respect the concerns that business owners and leaders may have about sharing financial information and believe that they should be able to begin sharing information based on their comfort level. They can certainly share more as this comfort level increases (and it usually does).

If financial statements are not enough, then where else do you need to turn your attention? To answer this, you must ask yourself, "What is it that really *creates* your financial performance? When you think about it, it comes down to two things: *the people in your organization and the stuff that they do.* When we considered this in Mexico, it was one of those "ah ha" moments for us. We thought, "Duh! What we really need to focus on are the most critical (and measurable) activities that people are engaged in every day and that ultimately drive our financial performance." Although you must focus on the endgame, in order to ensure that you have a winning score, you must focus on and measure the most critical activities that will accomplish this. In baseball, for example, a team must focus on runs, hits, errors, balls, strikes, walks, and a myriad of other measurable activities that impact the score. Although the same applies in business, the activities and measures are different. These are your KPIs.

Examples of Key Performance Indicators

Let's start with three of the most common and critical *lagging* financial measures:

- Revenue

- Gross margin

- Cash flow

I'd like you to imagine a scenario for a minute. Say you became enamored with the idea of focusing your employees on KPIs. And, say you have come to the conclusion that the most important KPI to focus on and improve in your organization is gross margin. So, with this in mind, you gather all of your employees together and say the following:

OK team, I've decided that I am going to engage all of you in driving the financial performance of this company and that you will all benefit by virtue of an incentive plan that I'm going to put in place. I've given it a lot of thought, and it's clear to me that the biggest opportunity for improvement here is gross margin—improving gross margin. All right, everyone, go do that!

What do you suppose the reaction to your little pep talk would be? What do you think the first question would be? If you said, "What the heck is gross margin?" you'd probably be right (and they might want to know what exactly is gross about it). My point is this: Of course you want to improve revenue, gross margin, and cash flow. But what are the measureable activities that must be addressed to ensure that these numbers improve? These are your leading KPIs.

So, let's drill down from each of the three lagging KPIs noted above. Table 4.1 displays a variety of leading KPIs from several companies I've worked with over the years. I'd like to point out that *you don't want this many KPIs.* These are simply examples. Some organizations make the mistake of going to the "key indicator buffet," as one of my clients so aptly put it. If you have too many measures, it's quite likely that none of them will get measured very well. Or, people will become overwhelmed and then paralyzed.

TABLE 4.1

Lagging KPI	Examples of Leading KPIs	Description
Revenue	Customer touches	Regular contact with existing customers (ideally face to face) to maintain relationships. Your best customer is the one you already have.
	Qualified leads	Prospective customers that have a reasonable likelihood of becoming actual customers. These prospects fit the profile of existing customers and/or would clearly benefit from your product or service.
	Sales calls	Number of contacts to qualified leads.
	Close rate (or win rate)	Percentage of leads that become customers.
	Average sale value	The average dollar amount of each sale. This will be driven in part by add-on sales and upselling.
	Number of demos	If demonstrating your product or service is a part of the sales cycle, this is a useful KPI. Note that this is only true if demos are done for qualified leads.
	Change orders	If the scope of the job increases, are the appropriate steps being taken (authorizations, etc.) to ensure that your company can invoice for them? Also, there might be an opportunity for change orders (add-on sales) that are identified by your salespeople or operations personnel.

TABLE 4.1 (continued)

Lagging KPI	Examples of Leading KPIs	Description
Cost of Goods Sold (or Cost of Sales)	Labor cost per unit produced	Labor dollars (typically just direct labor) divided by units produced.
	Overtime	Cost of overtime, or hours of overtime.
	Revenue per employee	Total revenue divided by total number of employees. This is a good high-level labor efficiency number that can often be compared to other businesses in your industry.
	Billable time	Percentage of hours worked that can be invoiced to customers. This is a critical number in most service businesses.
	Labor variance	The number of hours (or dollar value) in excess of estimated hours for a job (or less than estimate).
	Materials variance	Materials used in excess of estimate (or less than estimate).
	Warranty	Labor and/or materials cost of warranty work.
	Scrap	Materials that are wasted in the manufacturing process.
	Rework	Value of products and/or services that are unacceptable and must be fixed or replaced.
	Discounts	Value of discounts. More often than not, discounting is simply the result of bad sales habits. Every dollar of discounting comes right off the bottom line.

(continued)

TABLE 4.1 (continued)

Lagging KPI	Examples of Leading KPIs	Description
Cash Flow	Average collection days (sometimes called Days Sales Outstanding, or DSO)	Average number of days it takes to collect from customers after date of invoice.
	Aging	Dollar value of receivables from 0 to 30 days, 30 to 60 days, 60 to 90 days, etc. Aging is important due to reduced cash flow and also because the older a receivable becomes, the greater the potential of bad debt.
	Inventory turns	The number of times the value of inventory is sold in a year.
	Obsolete inventory	Dead or slow moving inventory.

How to Identify Your Key Performance Indicators

At Ownership Thinking, we begin the process of KPI identification with some research involving three forms of data gathering:

1. A five-year financial analysis

2. A survey of employees

3. An analysis of the competition

The purpose of the financial analysis is to identify strengths, weaknesses, trends, and opportunities. Though historical data like these are not the sole determinant of your KPIs, they are an important element.

FIVE-YEAR FINANCIAL ANALYSIS

Table 4.2 is an example of some historical data from a small manufacturing firm, which we will use as a case study in this chapter:

TABLE 4.2

	2005	2006	2007	2008	2009
Revenue	$23,255,210	$26,558,471	$30,985,850	$32,887,115	$21,884,844
Materials Cost	$9,767,188	$11,420,142	$13,478,844	$14,470,330	$10,285,766
Other Direct Expenses	$2,558,073	$3,028,664	$3,459,952	$3,910,889	$2,807,994
Gross Margin	$10,929,949	$12,109,665	$14,047,054	$14,505,896	$8,791,084
Gross Margin Percent	47.00%	45.60%	45.33%	44.11%	40.17%
Profit Before Taxes (PBT)	$1,930,182	$2,010,844	$2,218,586	$2,186,993	($205,772)
PBT as % of Revenue	8.30%	7.57%	7.16%	6.65%	–0.94%
Taxes	$752,771	$784,229	$865,249	$852,927	$0
Net Income	$1,177,411	$1,226,615	$1,353,337	$1,334,066	($205,772)
Net Income as % of Revenue	5.06%	4.62%	4.37%	4.06%	–0.94%
Current Assets	$3,880,398	$4,877,733	$6,406,993	$6,704,321	$6,393,509
Accounts Receivable	$2,421,090	$3,356,388	$4,454,712	$4,674,309	$4,346,722
Inventory	$1,057,054	$1,110,231	$1,678,854	$1,930,330	$1,887,877
Total Assets	$7,959,663	$8,890,733	$10,181,234	$11,209,699	$10,787,330
Current Liabilities	$2,114,489	$2,858,333	$3,480,580	$3,658,562	$3,932,587

TABLE 4.2 (continued)

	2005	2006	2007	2008	2009
Accounts Payable	$1,655,566	$2,098,511	$2,461,609	$2,645,463	$2,834,899
Long-Term Debt	$1,300,000	$1,151,900	$1,080,556	$958,704	$898,556
Equity	$3,335,572	$3,566,922	$3,486,000	$3,883,499	$3,434,567
Total Liabilities	$4,624,091	$5,323,811	$6,695,234	$7,326,200	$7,352,763
Depreciation	$28,895	$30,088	$29,561	$30,900	$31,216
Capital Expenditures	$66,892	$358,988	$251,875	$449,057	$0
Number of Employees	155	182	199	222	191
Cash Flow		$204,085	($244,170)	$506,838	$324,772
Current Ratio	1.84	1.71	1.84	1.83	1.63
Long-Term Debt	$1,300,000	$1,151,900	$1,080,556	$958,704	$898,556
Return on Assets	24.2%	22.6%	21.8%	19.5%	−1.9%
Collection Days	38	46	52	52	72
Inventory Turns	9.24	10.29	8.03	7.50	5.45
Revenue per Employee	$150,034	$145,926	$155,708	$148,140	$114,580

When creating a trend analysis, I suggest that you put the data in graph form. Graphs are generally the best method of looking at data when you want to quickly and easily identify year-to-year trends. Toward reducing the amount of pages spent here on analyzing these data, I will simply provide some insights based on the spreadsheet above:

- The most significant (and threatening) issue is the 33 percent drop in revenue in 2009 and the coinciding loss in profit. This dramatic drop in revenue was caused by the loss of only one client, which would suggest a lack of client diversity.

- Gross margin percentage (GM) had deteriorated every year, with the most significant drop in 2009. In researching this, it appeared that the owner and sales team had gotten into some sloppy bidding habits: discounting, giveaways, pricing errors, and so on. In addition, there were some inefficiencies in manufacturing that were having a negative impact on GM.

- Profit before tax had also been deteriorating. This was primarily due to the GM issues noted above, but also due to overstaffing on the administrative side (in overhead).

- Current ratio had dropped significantly in 2009, suggesting tight cash flow and potentially causing Accounts Payable issues. Current ratio is the ratio of current assets (assets that can be turned into cash within one year) to current liabilities (short-term debt obligations). In most industries, when this falls below 2.0, it is generally cause for some concern.

- Average collection days had increased very significantly, from 38 in 2005 to 72 in 2009. In an organization of roughly $30 million in annual sales, this increase of 34 days is the equivalent of $2 million in negative cash flow—a huge opportunity. The $2 million was arrived at by dividing the annual revenue in year 2009 by 365 (days in a year), then multiplying that number by 34 (the increase in average collection days from 2005 to 2009).

- Inventory turns declined from 2008 to 2009 by 2.05, which reflect another negative impact on cash flow of just over $500k.

- Revenue per employee tells us that the company did not react well to the decline in revenue for 2009 (as it relates to staffing).

SURVEY OF EMPLOYEES

The next step in data collection is what we call *intellectual data*, which we obtain through the use of a survey (generally completed by all employees, including leadership). There are actually two reasons for this survey (the details of which will be provided shortly). The first, of course, is to obtain data from employees that may assist the leadership team in identifying critical issues in the organization, which leadership might not be fully aware of. These issues can help to identify some of the relevant KPIs that the organization should focus on.

Engaging employees at this stage is important not only for the data, however. Companies are pretty good at starting initiatives, but often not very good at following through. If they don't engage their employees in the initiative from the get-go, there is really no ownership or buy-in from employees as it relates to the implementation (much less success) of the initiative. This results in leadership pushing the initiative down on everyone in the organization. My experience is that when leadership does this, employees resist or push back. Since the onus of success is now entirely on the shoulders of leadership, who obviously have a lot on their minds, the initiative typically will lose steam and ultimately will be abandoned. The real bummer here is that employees catch on to this and know that if they just wait long enough, most initiatives will indeed go away. The survey, then, is a mechanism to engage all employees in the initiative from the beginning, ensuring that they have an understanding of what is happening in the organization and have some ownership of the process and outcome.

The employee survey that we use at Ownership Thinking consists of two sections:

- The first is a series of statements that require a numbered response. This section provides us with a baseline of information regarding the organization's strengths and weaknesses relative to the four components of Ownership Thinking (right people, right education, right measures, right incentives).

- The second section consists of several open-ended questions, including the following:

  - What are the KEY, critical *operational* issues currently facing your company?

  - What are the KEY, critical *financial* issues currently facing your company?

  - What are the KEY, critical *people* issues currently facing your company?

  - What are two specific areas of opportunity for significant improvement?

  - Do you have any incentive plans in place? If so, what are the measures used to drive them, and are the incentives working?

Before I get into the survey data for the example company, it should be noted that the number of employees who respond to the survey is also a relevant data point. If the response rate is low (generally meaning less than 50 percent), this could indicate a couple of things: (1) The employees have been "oversurveyed" and may not have seen the results of those surveys or any changes related to them; or (2) Morale is low, and/or there is a general lack of trust in leadership or midlevel management, in which case it becomes important that the survey be confidential and that names not be associated with responses.

The survey results for this example company included the following responses, which were the common themes throughout the survey response data:

- Our revenue is deteriorating, and we had a huge drop in 2009 because we lost a big client.

- We lost money in 2009.

- We seem to be too reliant on the owner of the company as the primary "rainmaker." She also seems to be giving discounts to many of her long-term customers.

- Cash is tight—average collection days are not being controlled.

- We have too many employees on the administrative side—people are stepping on each other's toes, and there is a duplication of effort.

- Morale is poor.

- We haven't had any salary increases in two years.

- Our inventory control is not very good. We seem to be adding more and more inventory, and we have quite a bit of inventory that is not moving.

- Some of the production people have gotten kind of sloppy, and they are leaving the place in disarray for the next shift.

- We are having a lot of rework, sometimes because the equipment isn't functioning well; we need better preventative maintenance.

- Raw materials waste is not being tracked, but instead simply disposed of. I think things are getting worse because of that.

COMPETITIVE ANALYSIS

I typically don't put too much emphasis on competitive analysis when implementing Ownership Thinking in an organization. One reason is that, from my experience, organizations may limit their vision for success if they compare themselves to other companies in their industry, particularly if they are looking at "industry standards." If I do review industry standards with management teams when working through the KPI identification process, I am careful to point out that "this is what mediocre looks like."

It can be helpful, however, to review some competitive data to ensure that you are not significantly underperforming in certain areas or are so outpacing the competition in other areas that expecting too much more from your company might create unanticipated (and undesirable) consequences. On occasion, when doing competitive research, I may also come across a KPI that is common in an industry and that I may not have otherwise considered. The question now becomes, "Where do I get this data?" There are a variety of resources for getting competitive data for large, publically traded companies, but finding data for small, privately held companies can be a bit more difficult. I have had the best luck with the following:

- Trade associations for the industry in question, which will often do financial analysis of companies in the industry for their members.

- Trade magazines.

- Vendors, partners, and customers.

- Sageworks at www.profitcents.com. This is a Web-based tool that provides industry-standard data specifically for smaller, privately held companies.

The Key Indicator Workshop

Once these data have been collected, the next step in KPI identification is to get the leadership team together to sift through the data and arrive at the company's KPIs. This session typically lasts the better part of a day and should be held somewhere that will prevent any distractions. The facilitator of this meeting (preferably someone outside of the company who does not have a personal agenda) will guide the participants through the data and assist in tapping their knowledge of the company toward identifying the key, critical issues that the company is facing. These issues, then, can be translated into the relevant KPIs for the organization. The workshop that was held for our example company uncovered the following key issues:

- The company had several years of revenue growth, but there was a significant (and potentially life-threatening) drop in revenue in 2009 due to the loss of one large client.

- The company is too reliant on a few large customers.

- The company is too reliant on the owner of the company for sales.

- The sales team does not have an eye toward margin when it bids jobs. The team has fallen into some bad habits as it relates to discounting and not charging for everything that the client is receiving.

- Pricing is not standardized, and the sales team members are using different pricing models.

- Worker's compensation insurance has increased dramatically.

- Administrative costs are not being controlled, particularly labor.

- Cash flow is problematic, primarily due to collections and inventory management issues.

- Rework and scrap are having an impact on gross margin.

- Equipment downtime is affecting product turnaround and quality.

- There is an opportunity to improve labor efficiency on the production side.

- Based on the above analysis, the KPIs identified for our case study were as follows:

  - New Client Revenue and Existing Client Revenue and each of these as a Percentage of Total Revenue. This would highlight the importance of new revenue and client diversity. In addition, several operational metrics designed to drive revenue were identified, including Average Revenue per Client (for upselling), number of New Client Leads, number of Proposals to New Client Leads, and Close Rate.

  - Gross Margin and Profit Before Tax.

  - Discounts.

  - Labor and Materials Cost (above the Gross Margin line).

- Pricing Errors (or Order Entry Errors).

- Indirect Labor Cost as Percentage of Revenue.

- Labor Dollars per Ton Produced.

- Number of Incidents (Safety).

- Average Collection Days (or Days Sales Outstanding).

- Aging (dollar value of receivables at 0–30 days, 31–60 days, 61–90 days, and 91 days plus).

- Obsolete Inventory.

- Cycle Count Variance.

- Rework.

- Scrap or Waste.

- Equipment Utilization.

- Revenue per Employee.

At the conclusion of this workshop, it is quite common that the leadership team will have gone to the "key indicator buffet," identifying too many KPIs to effectively manage. The last thing that must be done in this workshop, then, is to identify which

KPIs the company will focus on and where. Some of the KPIs may not be important enough to focus on, or the information may not be available to track them effectively. These may be shelved permanently or temporarily. Others may be important, but perhaps not important enough to focus on at the leadership level (the primary purpose of the workshop is to build a leadership scoreboard). These KPIs may be used at the department, business unit, or location level. Only the most important and impactful KPIs should end up on the leadership scoreboard.

Creating the Scoreboard

Now that the KPIs have been identified, a scoreboard can be constructed for the leadership team to use for forecasting results. The scoreboard for our case study company can be seen in Table 4.3.

The final step in completing your scoreboard is to identify the people who will be forecasting for each KPI. When first considering this, it may appear obvious who should be assigned to each KPI; however, this is not always the case. The most common mistake I see is that the person identified to forecast a KPI is the person who has the *easiest access* to the number, as opposed to the *greatest influence over it*. In many, if not most, cases, the person with the easiest access to a number is the finance person (such as the CFO). If the CFO is forecasting every KPI, two things will occur: (1) employees will not learn about the KPI and what drives it, and (2) accountability for driving the KPI will fall on the shoulders of the CFO rather than the person who actually can improve it. It's

TABLE 4.3

XYZ Company		Month	Month	Month	Year to Date
Line Owners		Budget	Forecast	Actual	Budget
Name	Existing Customer Revenue				
Calculation	% of Total Revenue				
Name	New Customer Revenue				
Calculation	% of Total Revenue				
Calculation	Total Revenue	$0	$0	$0	$0
Name	Direct Labor Cost				
Name	Materials Cost	$0	$0	$0	$0
Name	Discounts and Adjustments				
Calculation	Cost of Goods Sold	$0	$0	$0	$0
Calculation	Gross Margin	$0	$0	$0	$0
Calculation	Gross Margin as % of Revenue				

(continued)

TABLE 4.3 (continued)

XYZ Company		Month	Month	Month	Year to Date
Name	Overhead				
Calculation	Profit Before Taxes (PBT)	$0	$0	$0	$0
Calculation	PBT as % of Revenue				
Operational KPIs					
Name	Average Revenue per Customer				
Name	Number of New Customer Leads				
Name	Number of Proposals to New Customers				
Name	Close Rate—New Customer Leads				
Name	$ Value of Pricing Errors				
Name	Admin Labor Cost % of Revenue				

TABLE 4.3 (continued)

XYZ Company		Month	Month	Month	Year to Date
Name	Labor $ per Ton Produced				
Name	Revenue per Employee				
Name	Recordable Incidents (Safety)				
Name	Cycle Count Variance				
Name	Obsolete Inventory				
Name	Rework				
Name	Scrap				
Name	Equipment Utilization				
Name	Average Collection Days				
	Aging	0–30 days	31–60 days	61–90 days	over 90 days
Name	AR Dollars				

important to remember that CFOs are the historians; they put the numbers together in a manner that allows us to understand them and make decisions based on historical data. They rarely actually "make the numbers happen." The people responsible for forecasting the KPIs, then, are the people who have the greatest influence over them. For example, the person reporting on existing customer revenue may be the sales manager, new customer revenue may be the business development manager, direct labor may be the production manager, and so on.

Utilizing the Scoreboard

Now that the scoreboard has been completed, it is time to begin using it in regular forecasting sessions, or huddles. As noted earlier, the primary purpose of conducting a huddle is to become more proactive in managing your KPIs, allowing the company to more effectively drive its financial performance and meet or exceed budget expectations. I suggest that you have two huddles a month and that they be held the first and third week of the month: same day, same time, and religiously. I like the first week because it will allow everyone to take a nice long view forward and will help in identifying issues early enough to do something about them. The third week is also good because most companies will have their actual financials from the previous month available at that time. The first few minutes of that huddle can be used to review the previous month's results and to compare those against budget and forecasts. After doing this, the huddle participants will reforecast for the current month.

Notice that there are three columns on the scoreboard for the current month, and three more for year-to-date (though we only show one in the model). The first column is the budget column, and the budget numbers should be populated prior to the huddle. The financial measures should come straight off of the organization's budget (hopefully created at the end of the previous year for the current year). The operational KPI budget numbers should be identified by the line owner and should be a legitimate stretch goal for that KPI. The second column is the forecast column (some companies call this an opinion, which I also like). This column will be populated, real time, during the huddle. I suggest that you assign someone to use the computer so that the scoreboard can be projected onto a screen using an LCD projector. Everyone whose name is on the scoreboard must attend this meeting (or, if some people can't go, someone from their area can attend in their absence). Starting at the top of the scoreboard, each "line owner" will give her forecast, meaning what she believes that number will actually be at month-end based on the realities of her area. For example, the first number being forecast is Existing Client Revenue. So, whoever is responsible for forecasting that number will provide the forecast for Existing Client Revenue. At the end of the meeting, when all of the KPIs have been forecast, everyone will have an idea of where the company is headed, what issues need to be addressed off line, and how to provide support to one another to improve things in problem areas. The third column is for the actuals, once they are available (again, this is typically midway through the following month). Remember that the objective is always to meet or exceed budget. This is not merely a reporting exercise.

One last note on huddles. Most companies are not very good at meetings. This is often because there is no agenda (or a bad one) and no data to support what will be discussed. Meetings often end up lengthy, disjointed, and emotional, where issues are rehashed and nothing of substance is achieved. Remember that your huddle is not about solving all of the issues that come up (or solving everyone else's issues, which people seem to enjoy), but instead simply *identifying where the company is*. With the level of visibility and accountability created by the huddles, and the fact that everyone must come back and re-report in two weeks, it is understood that people will go back and fix what needs to be fixed or improve what needs to be improved. Team members also begin to see clearly the associations between departments and may help one another get back on track where there are interdepartmental activities.

Huddle Guidelines

What follows is a variety of information that we provide to clients to ensure that they have effective forecasting sessions, or huddles.

DEFINITION

Huddles are short, to-the-point meetings where participants use the company's (or department's or business unit's) scoreboard to forecast results on a regular, formal basis.

OBJECTIVES OF HUDDLING

- The ultimate objective of utilizing scoreboards and forecasting is to meet or exceed goals. (*Note*: This is critically important. Many times, organizations will implement initiatives and then forget their reasoning. It then becomes, "we do this because we have to," which means that everyone thinks of it as busywork. The purpose of huddling is to meet or exceed goals; best-in-class companies do business this way.)

- To become more adept at forward thinking (forecasting) and less constrained by "rearview mirror" reactive management.

- To create an environment of high visibility and accountability.

- To identify issues early so that action can be taken.

- To create a learning environment, "a business of business people."

- To focus on the key, critical leading indicators that drive financial performance.

PARTICIPANTS IN HUDDLES

- In very small companies (15 employees or fewer), you may want to include everyone in the huddle, even if everyone does not have a number to forecast.

- In companies with 15 to a few hundred employees, the weekly or biweekly huddle will be attended typically by management only, although some companies choose to keep the meeting open to any employee who would like to observe. Departments or business units might have their own huddles prior to or after the management huddles.

- In companies with several hundred or even thousands of employees, scoreboards and huddles are more likely to be held at the business unit or department level.

GUIDELINES/SUGGESTIONS FOR EFFECTIVE HUDDLES

- Select a day and time that huddles will be held and stick to that schedule (for example: Tuesday mornings from 10 a.m. to 10:30 a.m. or the first and third Thursday of every month from 4 p.m. to 4:30 p.m.). The schedule should fit the pulse of your business.

- Huddles may be held every week or twice per month, but the numbers being forecast are always monthly forecasts, which are then updated or revised at each huddle. It's also important to have a year-to-date column on the scoreboard, since performance from month to month will fluctuate.

- *Important*: Do not have the forecast column already populated on the scoreboard prior to the huddle (to review only). Do not have your financial person forecast all of the numbers. Each line item should be owned by the person who has the greatest influence over that number, whether or not he has the easiest access to it. Line item owners should give their number, real time, at the meeting. We suggest that, during the huddle, someone use a computer to input the numbers as they are reported, and if you have an LCD projector, use it to project the scoreboard on a screen (if you do not have a projector, just use a monitor that can be seen by all participants). This real-time interaction is critical to identifying issues and creating an environment of accountability.

- Attending huddles and being prepared are nonnegotiable components of doing business if you are practicing Ownership Thinking. If you cannot be at a huddle (which will occur on occasion), then you must have someone there to represent you and your number(s).

- Have a specified agenda and time frame, and stay on task. On average, huddles should last no longer than 20 to 30 minutes (you might want to attach your huddles to already established management meetings). Remember that huddles are designed to identify where the company is and where it is heading so that action can be taken if necessary; this is not the time to debate or fix everything—that is done off line and in each participant's area of responsibility.

- For each huddle, identify a "cop" and a "scribe." The cop's responsibility is to recognize when the group has gotten off task or is going into too much detail on an issue, and to get the group back on track to finish on time. The scribe's responsibility is to take notes on key issues that need to be addressed off line and to forward that information to huddle participants in an e-mail after the meeting. These notes may be briefly reviewed at each huddle to ensure progress.

- Huddles are not just reporting mechanisms. They are designed to forecast results, to instigate change and improvement, and to celebrate wins. The ultimate objective is always to meet or exceed goals. Do not allow poor performance to go unaddressed (but no one gets shot!).

- When your actual results are available (typically midway through the following month), spend a few minutes at your huddle to review those against forecast and budget prior to forecasting for the current month. If actuals are significantly off target from forecasts, this should be addressed.

As opposed to departmental scoreboards, business unit or location scoreboards can be quite similar to the leadership scoreboard, as they are often focused on the same KPIs. If this is the case, then the scoreboard can be built with a separate tab (if using Excel) for each business unit or location, with the final tab being a "roll-up" of all business units or locations.

KPIs from Various Industries

The case study I've provided in this chapter is of a manufacturing firm. As I noted earlier in the book, however, the specific industry is irrelevant when it comes to implementing Ownership Thinking. My company has worked with virtually every industry over the past 15 years. The people are somewhat different, and the measures will be different, of course, but the methodology is basically the same. Given the fact that there will be people from many different industries reading this book , I am providing a list of KPIs that I've identified in various industries over the years.

- Construction

  - Number of bids

  - Win rate on bids

  - Backlog (contracted work that is not yet underway)

- Small-tool cost (small-tool shrinkage and damage can be significant in this industry)

- Change Orders

- Cost of disposal

- Buyout percent

- Number of safety accidents or violations

- Worker's compensation earned premium

- Plus or minus days to schedule variance

- Average number of items per punch list

- Equipment utilization

■ Retail

- Sales by category

- Inventory variance

- Number of cycle counts completed

- Sales per staff hour (very useful in scheduling, as well)

- Overtime (dollars and/or hours)

- Customer count

- Average ticket

- Clock-in errors

■ Restaurant

- Food cost

- Employee turnover

- Average check (average dollar amount per diner—a good measure of "upselling")

- Sales per staff hour

- Hourly payroll as percentage of sales

- Kitchen audit score

- Average comment card score

■ Technology Recycling Company

- Recycle, remarket, and service revenue

- Recycle pounds

- Recycle pounds per man-hour

- Number of assets processed

- Number of assets processed per man-hour

- Days to process recycling

- Remarket inventory dollars

■ Grower (plants and flowers)

- Labor dollars per flat produced (a *flat* is a group of plants)

- Shipping cost per flat

- Average number of trays per customer (to measure upselling)

- Scrap and spoilage

■ Software Company

- Sales by product group

- Percentage of sales from top 10 (customer diversity measure)

- Install margin

- Data conversion turn

- Call response time

- Renewal revenue per employee

- Number of demos

- Support labor dollars per incident

■ Distribution

- Catalogue contribution dollars from suppliers

- Returns and allowances

- Web sales

- Customers on electronic invoicing

- Picking errors

- Perfect order percent

- Trucking

  - Fuel surcharge

  - Freight rate revenue

  - Revenue per nondriver employee

  - Revenue miles per asset

  - Claims per 100k miles

  - Miles per gallon

  - Damage

  - Maintenance cost per mile

- Private School

  - Number of scholarships available

  - Number of tours

  - Number of students placed

  - Average class size

  - Student turnover

- Available financing

- Delinquent loans (dollars and number of)

■ Pest Control

  - Number of cancellations (and dollar value)

  - Commercial audit score

  - Residential audit score

  - Number of callbacks

  - Average duration of site visit

  - Percentage of clients on auto-pay

■ Landscaping

  - Revenue by area of service

  - Average revenue per crew per day

  - Number of callbacks

  - Warranty dollars

  - Shrink and damage

- **Parking Company**

  - Managed revenue

  - Leased revenue

  - Event revenue

  - Average contribution per location managed (and leased)

  - Number of new locations

  - Claims dollars

  - Number of delinquent monthlies

  - Field audit score

- **Mortgage Company**

  - Number of production agents

  - Average loan volume per agent

  - Number of returned files (and percent)

  - Average time to close

- Average time to final document

- Cost per loan

Departmental, Business Unit, and Location Scoreboards

As you now know, only the most important KPIs belong on a leadership scoreboard. These will be those KPIs that are driving companywide results at a fairly high level. There may be a number of KPIs that are important enough to measure on a regular basis, but, in fact, are supporting the higher level KPIs on the leadership scoreboard. These typically belong on a departmental scoreboard. For example, one of the most critical KPIs on the leadership scoreboard at Onions, Etc., the produce company mentioned in an earlier chapter, is Average Cost Per Package. This refers to the average cost of a package of onions when it is finished and ready to be shipped. There are several factors involved in managing that cost. The leadership team will not want to see that level of detail, however, and so there is a scoreboard on the shop floor at Onions, Etc., that focuses on the following KPIs that drive that number:

- Product waste

- Packaging waste

- Average setup time (packaging equipment)

145

- Packages per hour

- Overtime

Another great example of a departmental scoreboard is from Office Environments and Services (OES). When it first implemented Ownership Thinking, one of its key areas of opportunity was to get the sales team more focused on margin dollars and to help the team become better forecasters in general. We designed the following sales scoreboard with the sales team during that project (Table 4.4).

This is a very clever scoreboard, and it accomplishes a variety of things:

- It focuses each sales team member (each member has a scoreboard, and then the scoreboard rolls up) not only on revenue, but also on gross margin. There had been an inordinate amount of discounting and giveaways going on in the company, so using this reporting system helped to shine the spotlight on those issues. Discounting and providing giveaways may increase top-line revenue while actually decreasing gross margin. Commissions were also changed to be based on gross margin rather than revenue.

- It focuses the company on becoming more realistic with probabilities, particularly because every sales team member is able to see everyone else's scoreboard.

TABLE 4.4

Client	Invoice Amount	COGs (Including Commission)	G.P. ($)	Probability (%)	Estimated G.P. ($)	Estimated Bill Date	Jun	Jul	Aug
ABC	$10,000	$6,000	$4,000	100%	$4,000	15-Jun-03	$4,000	$0	$0
DEF	$12,000	$7,000	$5,000	100%	$5,000	15-Jul-03	$0	$5,000	$0
GHI	$6,000	$4,000	$2,000	100%	$2,000	20-Jul-03	$0	$2,000	$0
JKL	$18,000	$12,000	$6,000	60%	$3,600	25-Jul-03	$0	$3,600	$0
MNO	$4,000	$1,800	$2,200	75%	$1,650	30-Aug-03	$0	$0	$1,650

- It helps the company to be in tune with bill dates, which also helps the production people with scheduling. The gross margin amount is actually sent to the appropriate month and then added up so that a monthly gross margin amount can be accurately forecasted.

- The clients are color coded to show where the leads come from and to show when they pay their invoice (which will trigger commissions).

Sales scoreboards are quite important, as you might imagine. Additional KPIs for sales teams may include number of leads, close rate, number of proposals written, number of sales calls, average gross margin per sale, and so on. In addition, although salespeople generally are not excited about monitoring collections, it can be helpful if they do. At OE&S, salespeople are expected to monitor past due accounts and to report on them at their huddles.

┌─────────────────────────┐
KEY CONCEPTS
└─────────────────────────┘

- If you want to engage your employees in the financial performance of the company, using only financial statements is not enough.

- Full disclosure of financial information to all employees is not required to practice Ownership Thinking.

- In order to manage financial performance proactively, it is important to focus on leading, activity-based measures (Key Performance Indicators).

- Do not go to the "key indicator buffet." Trying to measure too many things leads to an overwhelmed staff, poor measurement, and, ultimately, the abandonment of the process.

- Involve your entire leadership team when identifying your KPIs, so that it has ownership of them.

- Huddles are about identifying where the company is headed, not about solving every issue. They should take no more than 20 to 30 minutes, and issues that are identified should be addressed off-line.

- Do not go into too much minutia with the leadership scoreboard. Lower-level KPIs can be placed on departmental, business unit, or location scoreboards.

CHAPTER FIVE

Get RIP'd: Rapid Improvement Plans

W e often use the phrase "share the insomnia" in our work at Ownership Thinking because we want every employee in our client organizations to be thinking about, and acting on, the important issues—the issues that may in fact keep the owners awake on occasion. To be 100 percent effective, Ownership Thinking must be drilled all the way through the organization, from both top to bottom and bottom to top. When working with companies, I use the concept and language of "cascading" to drive this point home. Figure 5.1 is a good visual of this concept.

Most people think of a waterfall when they hear the word *cascading*. I like to use this image when considering the different levels of engagement of Ownership Thinking. The top of a waterfall, higher than the rest of the waterfall and typically narrower, correlates to the long-term, high-level thinking that guides the organization's decision making. As noted in the figure, this would

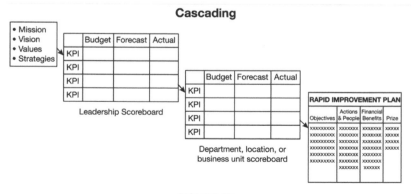

Cascading

FIGURE 5.1

include your mission, vision, values, and key strategies. The next level of the business waterfall is a bit broader, more involved, and more tactical. This would be the leadership scoreboard, as discussed in the previous chapter. Below that would be departmental, location, or business unit scoreboards. Finally, at the base of the waterfall you have your Rapid Improvement Plans (RIPs), where everyone in the organization becomes engaged.

The objective of a RIP is to attack and improve one Key Performance Indicator (KPI) at a time with a high-involvement, detailed plan. The title of this chapter actually came from Marich Confectionary, a candy company that created a theme and logo around the creation of RIPs with a picture of a body builder and the slogan "Get RIP'd." Every employee in your organization can participate in RIPs, although not everyone will necessarily participate in *every* RIP. In other words, some RIPs might be company-wide and others might be departmental in nature (that is, focusing on one department or business unit). The steps to creating RIPs are as follows:

1. Identify a Key Performance Indicator that needs improvement.

2. Identify a quantifiable goal and a time frame for the RIP (typically 90 days).

3. Quantify the financial benefit of reaching the goal.

4. Determine the actions and people required to achieve the goal.

153

5. Name the RIP and create a theme (have some fun).

6. Identify a celebration for reaching the goal.

RIP Case Study

In order to help you understand this process, I will provide examples highlighting each of these steps. This first example of a RIP was created within an asphalt company having about $25 million in annual revenues and roughly 150 employees. The company's core business is producing and laying asphalt for parking lots and other areas, as well as doing some roadwork and repairs. The first KPI that this organization attacked with a RIP was rework. It's a good example to use here because rework is a very common issue in most organizations, regardless of the industry. This example is particularly interesting because of the disconnect between leadership and employees around this issue that came to light as I worked with the company. I had completed the management team work in the company (leadership training, identification of KPIs, scoreboard design, and incentive plan design) and was facilitating the first of several employee training sessions. Early in the session, I was reviewing the scoreboard with the employees so that they could see the KPIs that had been identified for the company and have some sense of the direction that the company was headed in this regard. Rework was one of the KPIs on the scoreboard, and before I got to that point, one of the employees spoke up and said, "What does rework mean?" So I asked him, "Do you ever make a mistake on a job and have to return to fix it?" He responded, "Sure, it happens all the time. Maybe we covered a manhole, or there was some finish work not completed, or the grading was poor." I said, "That's rework."

I'll never forget the response that I got from this employee. He said, "I thought that was customer service." Customer service! How on earth could anyone think *that* you might ask. Well, in this company it had historically been emphasized that the customer was always right and that the customer always came first. Of course, this is a very important message, but apparently there was another message missing, which was "do it right the first time, because there is a cost associated to any rework that must be done." Well, now I was curious, and I asked this group of employees what percentage of their jobs they had to return to in order to perform "customer service." The response staggered me—it was roughly 70 percent! So, what employees evidently thought to be a good thing was costing this company about $300k a year in labor and materials (not to mention the opportunity cost).

Using this example as a guide, here are the steps to take to design a RIP:

1. IDENTIFY A KEY INDICATOR THAT NEEDS IMPROVEMENT

The criteria for selecting a KPI to build a Rapid Improvement Plan around (in this case, it was rework) are typically as follows:

- The KPI can be found on the scoreboard.

- The KPI should be having a significant effect on the organization's financial performance.

- The KPI usually should be common enough where most employees can participate in it. This doesn't always need to be the case, however. RIPs can be department, location, area, or business-unit specific. I suggest that you always think through this when designing the plan. Many times what may seem specific to one department or a few people is actually touched by many departments and people. A good example of this is average collection days (average number of days it takes to collect from customers after invoicing). At first glance, this would seem to be an accounting issue only. By asking the right question, however, it becomes clear that many people actually affect it. The question in this example is: "Why aren't our customers paying us on time?" And the answer includes nearly every department: Customers might not be paying because the salesperson did not relay the terms correctly or wrote a poor contract. They might not be paying because they are unhappy with the quality of the product or service. Customers might not be paying because the product or service might have been partially filled or completed, or it might have been late. There might be some inaccuracy in invoicing or documentation. We simply might not have asked, and so on.

- If you are new to Ownership Thinking, I sometimes suggest that the first one or two RIPs be chosen, in part, because there is a strong likelihood of success. It's nice to get a win or two under your belt quickly. People become addicted to success, and this will help to get Ownership Thinking off to a good start.

2. IDENTIFY A QUANTIFIABLE GOAL AND A TIME FRAME FOR THE RIP

It is important to identify a quantifiable goal for the RIP to ensure that the organization can tell when the goal is reached. I suggest that you do not get too fancy here. Identify something that people can relate to and that does not require sophisticated technology or accounting systems to calculate. The metric that our asphalt company chose was percentage of jobs requiring rework, and the goal was to reduce this from its current 70 percent to 30 percent. In other words, by doing X, Y, and Z correctly the first time, employees agreed that they could reduce rework incidents by this percentage.

The time frame I generally suggest for a RIP is 90 days. This is long enough for organization members to significantly affect a KPI, but not so long that they lose interest. Remember that the goal is to create "rapid improvement." On occasion, there may be a KPI that requires more time to tackle, in which case the time frame can be set at six months. Another way to approach this kind of KPI is to have two escalating goals. For example, we might commit to reduce return visits by 20 percent in the first three months and a total of 40 percent in six months. If this is done, then there might be two celebrations (this will be explained in step six later in this chapter).

3. QUANTIFY THE FINANCIAL BENEFIT OF
REACHING THE GOAL

In order to ensure that the RIP is worth the time and effort to pursue, I suggest that the numbers be "crunched" to discover what the financial effect on the company would be if the goal were to be met (and to make sure that pursuing the RIP outweighs any cost associated with implementing it). In the asphalt company we are using as an example, it was determined that by reducing rework from 70 to 30 percent, the annual cost savings would amount to approximately $200k. This was determined by calculating the average expense of one rework incident, multiplying that times the number of incidents that would be reduced during the RIP, and then extrapolating that over a full year. As we noted earlier in the book, virtually all of the savings will fall right to the bottom line. And remember, it is always a good idea to ask employees how much revenue it would take to get that $200k to the bottom line. If the organization historically had a 5 percent profit, for example, it would take $4 million in revenue to bring $200k to the profit line. This is calculated by dividing the cost savings by the profit percent ($200k divided by .05). Clearly this RIP is worth pursuing.

4. DETERMINE THE ACTIONS AND PEOPLE
REQUIRED TO ACHIEVE THE GOAL

I suggest that this not be a management exercise only. Rather, the employees who touch this issue on a regular basis should be tapped to create the RIP (with the help of perhaps one person from management). This is important for two reasons. First, these employees are living with the issue day in and day out, and will likely have insights that management will not. In addition, this creates employee involvement and buy-in and promotes learning. In this example, the four areas that appeared to have the biggest effect on rework were manufacturing (of the asphalt), bidding, grading (preparing the ground), and field personnel who were actually laying the asphalt. In a brief, two-hour session with a representative from each of these four areas, it was determined that the primary causes of rework were as follows:

- There was an intermittent problem with one of the raw materials that was causing the asphalt to dry out too soon on some jobs.

- The bidding department owned up to the fact that it had been making more mistakes on bids than in the past, which often translated to mistakes in the field. This is a good example of the Adult Contract, by the way. The department was comfortable bringing up the fact that it had been making more errors because it knew its employees would not "get shot."

- The employee involved in grading pointed out that the grading equipment was not being calibrated frequently enough, creating a base that at times was not level.

- The person representing the field noted that sometimes when a team arrived at a job site, not all of the tools that it needed were on the truck, requiring a trip back to the shop to retrieve them (or perhaps buy them if the team was in a remote location).

Based on this analysis, it was determined that the following activities should be put into practice:

- The manufacturing representative would look into the raw material problem and either would work with the current supplier to get that raw material consistently up to spec or would source a new supplier.

- The representative from the bidding department decided to create a RIP specific to that department to reduce bidding errors.

- The grading representative suggested that a grease board be set up in the shop to identify all the pieces of grading equipment and the dates they should be calibrated, and that the service department would stick to that schedule.

- The representative from the field decided to create a simple tool inventory form for each truck and to use that to do a quick inventory of each truck at the end of the workday (when it was slow) to ensure that teams would have what they needed the following morning (when everyone is very busy).

As you can see, this is not brain surgery. Employees typically see the issues involved and can come up with solutions. Also note that this is not an extremely time-consuming process. Typically, a RIP can be designed in a matter of a few hours.

5. NAME THE RIP AND CREATE A THEME

Now it's time to bring the RIP to life. To do this, I suggest that the RIP be given a (hopefully clever) name and that a theme be attached to it. The name given to the RIP outlined here is: Redo Is Doo Doo. A bit goofy, perhaps, but the employees thought it was fun. A large scoreboard was created around this theme, with the various areas of activity highlighted and regularly updated, and it was posted in the shop and vehicle area of the company. More examples are provided later in this chapter.

6. IDENTIFY A CELEBRATION FOR REACHING THE GOAL

This is a very important step and is often underemphasized in companies practicing Ownership Thinking. A celebration should be identified *at the beginning of the RIP* that will be carried out if the goal is met. In the case of Redo Is Doo Doo, the celebration was a breakfast for everyone in the organization. They did, in fact, reach the goal in 90 days, and all 150 employees got together a bit early one day to celebrate. They had a table full of breakfast burritos and had tucked $20 bills inside 20 of the burrito wrappings, which added to the fun. The total cost of this celebration was approximately $750.

At this point, you might be thinking, "OK, everyone participated in this RIP, which brought $200,000 to the bottom line, and each employee got a burrito? And, maybe $20? That hardly seems fair!" It's important to keep in mind that the breakfast was simply a celebration of the win. The real payoff for employees is the potential effect on their incentive plan. In this company, 30 percent of profit dollars that surpassed its minimum threshold (an important point) was going toward the incentive plan. Given that the minimum threshold was surpassed, the real effect was an additional $60k to the incentive plan. This is a very powerful tool to engage employees in funding their incentive plan, while simultaneously ensuring that the plan does not become an entitlement.

As you can see, RIPs are incredibly powerful (yet simple) tools and accomplish the following in an organization:

- They create significant financial improvements in a short period of time.

- They help to identify process improvements.

- They fund the incentive plan.

- They create new standards of performance.

- They are great training opportunities.

- They are fun! I like to think of these as *real* team building. In other words, they are having a measurable effect on the organization, as opposed to many team-building activities that, frankly, are just fluff.

What follows are several more examples of Rapid Improvement Plans that our clients have implemented over the years.

RIP Example 1:
No More Tears

This RIP was created for an organization that packages and sells produce and that was doing roughly $20 million in annual revenues. One of the most critical KPIs at the company is average cost per package, that is, the average cost of a package of produce when it leaves the facility. The company's first RIP was to reduce average cost per package from $2.00 to $1.50. Here are the details:

- KPI: Average Cost per Package.

- Quantifiable Objective: To reduce Average Cost per Package by 50 cents in 90 days.

- Financial Effect on the Company: Astonishingly, this added $600k to the company's profit over a period of one year, which significantly affected the incentive pool.

- Actions:

  - Move to 70 percent purchasing from one supplier (with which they created a partnership relationship).

163

- Improve prepack inspection process.

- Calibrate packing equipment according to new schedule.

- Reduce overtime by 60 percent. (*Note:* This can often be a touchy issue, since overtime is often coveted. If this is the case in your company, this action may simply have to be mandated. It is also true that, in many cases, incentive payouts will make up for most or all of the lost overtime compensation.)

- Reduce average equipment set-up time to 30 minutes.

- Repair and maintain labeler.

- Use new scheduler software.

■ Name: No More Tears (one of their primary products is onions).

■ Celebration: Barbeque and band.

■ Total Cost: $1,800 (which was the cost of the celebration and some costs related to the process improvements noted above).

RIP Example 2:
The Big Green Cash Cow

This was a RIP designed to reduce average collection days in a manufacturing company with approximately $7 million in annual revenues.

- KPI: Average Collection Days.

- Quantifiable Objective: To reduce Average Collection Days by 20 (from 60 to 40) in 90 days.

- Financial Effect on the Company:

  - Increase available cash by $600,000.

  - Increase GM (annually) by $20,000, since the cash is now available to take discounts that suppliers offer with early payment to them.

  - Reduce interest expense by paying down debt ($24,000 in annual interest savings).

- Actions:

  - Produce clear, accurate, and timely invoices.

  - Ask for deposits and/or progress payments.

165

- Introduce a seven-day customer service phone call (seven days after shipment and invoicing, representatives from customer service would call customers to ensure that they were happy with the products and service and to ask if there were any questions about the invoice). This is a great example of some of the creative process improvements that come about with RIPs. This was a call that customers would consider a positive follow-up, yet it resulted in discovering and/or eliminating the potential of excuses for nonpayment of the invoice.

- Complete credit approvals prior to manufacturing the order.

- Create and send (by e-mail) monthly statements to customers.

- Have the sales team keep track of past due invoices and report on these at each huddle, after which the next action to take would be determined.

- Improve quality and fill rate (it was determined that some of the nonpayment issues were due to quality issues and incomplete orders).

■ Name: The Big Green Cash Cow (the scoreboard was a big green cow up on the wall in the lunchroom, with all of the activities tracked on it).

166

- Celebration: Ice cream social.

- Total Cost: $300.

RIP Example 3:
Wash Away Warranty Work

This RIP was designed in an organization that provides painting services to commercial and residential buildings and homes. The goal was to reduce warranty work (cost) that was caused by errors (wrong color, poor quality of paint or stain, and so on).

- KPI: Warranty Cost.

- Quantifiable Objective: To reduce Warranty Cost by 50 percent.

- Financial Effect on the Company:

  - Decrease labor and material costs by $13,000 per month ($156k annually).

  - Free up labor being used on warranty work for income-generating work and/or sales calls.

  - Increase incentive pool by $36k per year (if minimum threshold is met).

- Improve customer service.

- Increase potential for repeat business.

■ Actions:

- Receive clear, accurate scope of work from the bidding department.

- Improve handoff documentation from project manager to operations.

- Conduct job review meetings with crew leaders and project managers to improve communications.

- Identify best practices and create standard operating procedures.

- Hold a training session on the handoff process from project manager to crew leader.

- Create and implement an internal prepunch list walk-through.

■ Name: Wash Away Warranty Work.

■ Celebration: Pizza party.

■ Total Cost: $600.

RIP Example 4:
Grand Slam

This RIP was designed to increase the average sale in a chain of retail hardware stores.

- KPI: Average Sale (total sales divided by number of transactions).

- Quantifiable Objective: To increase Average Sale by 4 percent in 90 days.

- Financial Effect on the Company:

  - Increase revenue by $200,000 ($800k annually).

  - Increase profit before tax by $98,000 (annual).

  - Increase incentive pool by $26,000 (if threshold is met).

  - Drive equity value (they had an Employee Stock Ownership Program).

- Actions:

  - Identify best-selling products and merchandise accordingly.

- Have daily "employee specials."

- Allow employees to identify their favorite products and to post signs for them (for example, Susan recommends this!).

- Conduct monthly training sessions provided by suppliers.

- Provide extraordinary customer service to all customers and make them aware of additional products that may interest them.

- Sell solutions, not just products.

- Monitor results by teams.

- Provide various home repair or improvement classes for customers.

■ Name: Grand Slam (the theme was baseball, and the scoreboard was a baseball diamond).

■ Celebration: BBQ and baseball game.

■ Total Cost: $2,200.

RIP Example 5:
Yabba Dabba Doo

The following is a RIP designed to reduce rental and fuel costs in an athletic field construction company that installs world-class synthetic and natural turf playing systems around the world.

- KPI: Rental and Fuel Costs.

- Quantifiable Objective: To save 12 percent off of budgeted Rental and Fuel Costs.

- Financial Effect on the Company: $16,500.

- Actions:

  - Return equipment in a timely fashion.

  - Rent only as a last resort (use owned equipment first).

  - Return full of fuel.

  - Use tax-free off-road fuel.

  - Call off rent ASAP.

- Name: Yabba Dabba Doo.

- Celebration: Lunch for everyone.

- Cost: $25 per person, total of $600.

RIP Example 6:
Surf and Turf

Another RIP from the same company:

- KPI: Credit Card Rebates.

- Quantifiable Objective: To obtain $1,000,000 in purchases using the PNC–Visa card between 6/1/09 and 8/31/09.

- Financial Effect on the Company: Rebate of 70 basis points, or $14,000.

- Actions:

  - Have all employees use PNC–Visa for project materials and incidentals.

  - Approach all vendors not currently paid with VISA to see if they accept VISA, and if so, convert them.

- Name: Surf and Turf.

- Celebration: Lobster bake on a Friday afternoon in August in the corporate office parking lot or shop lot.

- Cost: $35 per head ($750 to $1,000).

RIP Example 7:
Double Your Pleasure,
Double Your Fun

This RIP was focused on increasing the percentage of multiple-unit sales in a chain of salons. It was designed to promote upselling of retail hair and beauty products, as measured by the percentage of sales that had more than one product involved.

- KPI: Multiple-Unit Sales.

- Quantifiable Objective: To increase the percentage of Multiple-Unit Sales (sales with more than one product) from its current 22 percent to 30 percent.

- Financial Effect on the Company:

  - $152k in annual revenue.

  - $70k in additional profit before tax.

  - Roughly $20k in additional incentive payouts to employees.

173

- Actions:

  - Create a "Privileged Customer Program," or PCP.

  - Give customers a free membership to the PCP with any multiple-product purchase.

  - Create a scoreboard to be displayed in the lunchroom with daily goals and results.

  - Educate employees on families of products so they can promote products that are meant to be used together.

  - Promote travel-size products.

  - Demonstrate products when styling hair (show and tell).

- Name: Double Your Pleasure, Double Your Fun.

- Celebration: Softball game and BBQ.

- Cost: $500.

RIPs in Action: Mercedes Medical

One of the most exciting and innovative examples I've seen of RIP design, implementation, and financial improvement comes from Mercedes Medical, a medical products distributor in Florida. I generally suggest one or two RIPs per quarter; however, the employees at Mercedes identified RIPs as the core of practicing Ownership Thinking in their organization and have approached it in a very disciplined yet fun and interactive fashion. During the first year of practicing Ownership Thinking, the employees completed nearly 20 RIPs. And they had a blast doing it. Every quarter, the employees have a meeting to review the results of RIPs that have recently been completed and to introduce new ones for the upcoming quarter. They are big into themes, so, for example, one of their RIPs was to increase Web sales, and the theme was The Matrix (as in the movie). They create movielike posters for each RIP (with pictures of employees instead of actors) and have a skit to introduce it. For The Matrix, an employee, dressed as Morpheus, started the skit by saying to the audience: "Welcome people of Zion," and then took them through the details of the RIP. The employees were clearly enjoying the RIPs and the hoopla surrounding them, but were also enjoying the bonus checks. Table 5.1 demonstrates the financial impact of RIPs at Mercedes Medical through the third quarter of its first year practicing Ownership Thinking.

TABLE 5.1

QTR	Name	Objective	Savings
Q1	The Vendor Love Boat	Reduce junk fees; take all discounts	$30,000.00
Q1	Sizzlin' Samples	Reduce samples expense and sample freight	$12,000.00
Q1	Mercedes Drives 100	Add 100 new accounts per month	$11,954.00
Q1	Returns of the Jedi	Reduce customer returns	$15,000.00
Q1	It Ain't Easy Being Green	Reduce carbon footprint	$5,000.00
Q2	CPR Flatliners	Reduce customer attrition	$15,325.00
Q2	The Terminator	Paperless picking and packing in warehouse	$5,400.00
Q2	Deal or No Deal	Reduce various operating expense	$17,500.00
Q2	UP (a catalog adventure)	Obtain vendor sponsorships for ads in catalog	$41,000.00
Q2	Credit Casino Royale	Reduce customer credits due to order error	$12,500.00
Q3	The Matrix	Increase Web sales	$54,000.00
Q3	No Going Postal	Invoices via fax or e-mail; reduce postage	$441.76
Q3	The Three Amigas	Upsell customers during order taking	$3,583.00
			$223,703.76

RIP Tips

Rapid Improvement Plans are one of the most critical and influential components of practicing Ownership Thinking. And yet, I often see them fall by the wayside. Here are a few tips to (hopefully) ensure that you stick with them.

- Your Ownership Thinking Steering Committee (explained in Chapter 7) should probably be in charge of ensuring that RIPs are created and executed.

- The biggest problem with creating RIPs is that people overthink them. They turn them into something very ominous and complicated. They are actually quite easy to design. Once you have identified the KPI that will be focused on, start by getting the appropriate people together and asking the question: "Why aren't we performing as well as we should on this KPI?" Then it's simply about identifying the problem areas and coming up with solutions for each one (refer to the questions I asked earlier about why customers don't pay on time).

- Make sure that RIPs are formalized and documented.

- Bring them to life! Name them, create a theme, and devise a highly visible mechanism for tracking and communicating results.

- The results should be monitored and reported throughout the RIP, not just at its completion.

- Don't forget to celebrate the wins! I suggest that, even if a RIP is departmental, the celebration for it should be companywide for the following reasons:

  - Ultimately, every RIP is about driving company results, which affects everyone's incentive plan.

  - It is an opportunity for people to learn about other areas of the company and how those areas affect everyone.

- It is good for team building.

KEY CONCEPTS

- Rapid Improvement Plans are a tool to engage all employees in improving the performance of one KPI at a time.

- RIPs are not difficult to design and can typically be created in a matter of a few hours.

- Nonmanagement personnel should be involved in the design of RIPs.

- Your organization should always have at least one RIP in process.

- RIPs are very powerful tools for a number of reasons aside from profit enhancement. They also identify process improvements, fund the incentive plan, are great training mechanisms, and are fun.

CHAPTER SIX

Employee Stock Ownership Plans (ESOPs): Do Ownership Thinkers Have to Own?

I am a board member of the National Center for Employee Ownership (NCEO), a private, nonprofit membership and research organization that serves as the nation's leading source of accurate, unbiased information on Employee Stock Ownership Plans (ESOPs) and other equity compensation plans, such as stock options. This includes synthetic equity plans, such as Stock Appreciation Rights (SARs) and phantom stock. In my opinion, the NCEO is the leading organization of its type in the United States, and I am proud to be associated with it.

The founder of the NCEO is Corey Rosen, and I want to thank him for his help with the technical aspects of ESOPs as described in this chapter. In addition to having an extensive education in this area and 30 years as the executive director of the NCEO, Corey worked as a professional staff member in the U.S. Senate, where he helped draft some of the legislation governing employee ownership. Corey is also a friend and supporter of mine and of Ownership Thinking, and I have turned to him many times over the years for his knowledge and assistance in matters concerning ESOPs and other equity plans. There are many misconceptions—and much misinformation—out there on these subjects, and if you want unbiased and well-researched information about them, I suggest that you contact the NCEO at www.nceo.org.

This book is about how to create an ownership culture and why it is important to do so. However, I do not mean to imply that a company must actually share equity in order to have an ownership culture. I would estimate that less than 10 percent of our clients over the years have broad-based equity plans, so it should be quite clear that a company that practices Ownership Thinking need not share equity with its employees. I believe I can safely say, however, that if a company has a broad-based equity plan (such as an ESOP), the company needs to practice Ownership Thinking and the principles outlined in this book, in order to maximize the potential benefits of the plan.

Statistically, companies with ESOPs *and* Ownership Thinking cultures significantly outperform not only their previous years' performance but also the performances of their non-ESOP competitors. ESOP companies that don't do this cultural work, however, actually underperform. This is often due (at least in part) to unrealistic expectations that are created among employees when an ESOP is introduced and employees are not taught what an ESOP is and, perhaps more important, what it is not. Fundamentally, an ESOP is a retirement plan tied to the value of a company's equity; it is nonvoting stock. Given this, it does not connote shared control or consensus management. As I noted earlier, Ownership Thinking is not synonymous with democracy. The same could be said for an ESOP.

Technical Aspects of ESOPs

ESOPs provide a way for companies to use tax-deductible contributions to an ESOP trust to buy out an existing owner or owners, help finance growth in pretax dollars, or provide an employee benefit through the contribution of shares to the plan. Tax benefits of an ESOP include the following:

- Owners in closely held C corporations can defer taxation on the gain they make selling to an ESOP, provided certain requirements are met.

- Companies can borrow money through an ESOP for any business purposes and repay it in pretax dollars.

- Companies contributing stock to an ESOP get a tax deduction for its fair market value.

- In C corporations, dividends used to repay an ESOP loan or passed through to employees are tax deductible.

- In S corporation ESOPs, the profits attributable to the trust are exempt from federal and, usually, state income tax.

- From the employee perspective, ESOPs are almost always funded through corporate contributions, not through the employees' own purchase of shares. Employees are not taxed when contributions are put into the trust, paying tax instead only when they take their account balances out of the ESOP or if they roll the balance into an IRA or other retirement plan, when the balances come out of that plan.

As beneficial as ESOPs can be, however, they are not right for every company. ESOPs have very specific rules about who is in the plan, how much those people get, and when they get it.

ESOPs do not allow for companies to make discretionary choices about these issues beyond what is allowed by these rules, most of which are the same or very similar to rules for other tax-qualified retirement plans. In fact, ESOPs are governed by the same law—the Employee Retirement Income Security Act—as pension plans, profit-sharing plans, 401(k) plans, and similar arrangements. They usually do not work well in companies that are not profitable, that lack successor management where an owner is being bought out, that are too small to absorb the costs of setting up and maintaining a plan (generally under 15 employees), or that have management that never gets comfortable with the idea that as owners, employees will expect more information and more serious attention to their ideas.

Employees do not usually contribute to the ESOP; rather contributions are funded by the company as a benefit, and shares are allocated to employee accounts on a nondiscriminatory basis, much as in a profit-sharing plan. Generally, in an ESOP company, all employees over the age of 21 who work more than 1,000 hours in a plan year must be included in the next plan year. Shares are allocated to individual employee accounts based on relative compensation, and the allocated shares are subject to vesting. If the plan provides for vesting all at once, called *cliff vesting*, employees must be 100 percent vested after three years of service; if vesting is gradual, it must not be slower than 20 percent after two years and 20 percent per year more until 100 percent is reached after six years. A faster vesting schedule applies where the ESOP contribution is used as a match to employee 401(k) deferrals.

When employees reach age 55 and have 10 years of participation in the plan, the company must either give them the option of diversifying 25 percent of their account balances among at least three other investment alternatives or simply pay the amount out to the employees. At age 60, with 10 years of service, employees can have 50 percent diversified or distributed to them.

When employees retire, die, or become disabled, the company must distribute their vested shares to them not later than the last day of the plan year following the year of their departure. For employees leaving before reaching retirement age, distribution must begin no later than the last day of the sixth plan year following their year of separation from service. Payments can be made in substantially equal installments out of the trust over five years, or they can be made in a lump sum. With the installment method, a company normally pays out a portion of the stock from the trust each year.

Closely held companies and some thinly traded public companies must repurchase the shares from departing employees at their fair market value, as determined by an independent appraiser. This so-called put option can be exercised by the employee in one of two 60-day periods, one starting when the employee receives the distribution and the second period one year after that. The employee can choose which one to use. This obligation should be considered at the outset of the ESOP and be factored into the company's ability to repay the loan.

What has been described here are the basics of an ESOP. I've included the details in part to make the point that there is a lot to an ESOP from a technical standpoint, and, therefore, it is important to get legal and financial advice if you are interested in pursuing one. Again, the NCEO is a great source of information and resources for this.

Cultural Considerations of ESOPs

Remember that merely creating an ESOP in your organization will not create an ownership culture. One of the best examples of this that I can give you is a client I first worked with in 2005, an international technical engineering consulting firm that focuses on commercial building systems. At the time, the company was over 50 years old and had been 100 percent ESOP for many years. The ESOP was put into place by the founder of the company, who clearly had good intentions and perhaps meant the transaction to be a magnanimous gesture to the employees. He was known to say that the employees did not exist for the benefit of the company, but rather the company existed for the benefit of the employees. Employees became owners by virtue of the ESOP with no understanding of what it meant to be an owner and no education as to the financial implications of the ESOP or what it takes for an organization to sustain itself and grow in a competitive environment. In other words, there was no reciprocity.

When I began working with this company, the trend analysis we did showed a profit before tax averaging between 2 and 3 percent for the five years prior to our engagement (with one of those years showing a significant loss). Based on my experience and on industry trends, the company should have been running closer to 10 percent or more. Due to the lack of business acumen among employees, and the philosophy expressed by the founder, virtually all profits had been distributed to employees, so nothing was left for strategic growth. In addition, since employees did not really understand the financial ramifications of their decisions and demands, they made decisions and demands that were, in fact, damaging to their company. If this had not been addressed and reversed with Ownership Thinking, it is entirely possible that the company would not be in existence today, and then the equity that employees relied on for retirement would be worth nothing. This is a perfect example of entitlement thinking that can ultimately "kill the goose that lays the golden eggs."

Steve Langley, CEO of Osborne Industries, expressed some similar concerns about his company in a recent conversation I had with him. He noted that when the company went from 30 to 100 percent ESOP in 2007, there was a tremendous amount of excitement among employees. Since there was really no business acumen training when the ESOP occurred or training around the ESOP itself, employees soon were simply waiting to see what would change rather than being a part of the change themselves. The executive team at Osborne made the same mistake that many ESOP companies make, which was to believe that (1) everyone in the company would have the same level of understanding about ownership that it had, and (2) the ESOP itself would create cultural change. It wasn't until leadership began educating and engaging employees in the business that they began to see the cultural change they were hoping for.

As owner and consultant at Workplace Development Inc., my friend Cathy Ivancic has provided communication, education, and organizational development services to companies with ESOPs for more than 7 years and has been in the field for more than 20 years. Cathy is often approached by business owners and leaders who have created an ESOP and are frustrated because "it should be working, but just isn't." Again, they probably assumed that the plan would change behavior, when, in fact, it did not. She has also told me that business owners who transfer ownership to an ESOP often retain a patriarchal attitude after the transfer. In other words, they still believe that it is their responsibility, as they did before the ESOP, to take care of their employees. They might, in fact, become angry not only that things have not changed, but also that their employees don't seem to be grateful for what the owners have done for them. She helps employees to understand that the real value is in the creation of an engaged culture that will support the ESOP and its members, and not in the ESOP itself.

Another interesting viewpoint on this topic comes from Mike Rydin, CEO of HCSS, whom I've mentioned a few times in this book. HCSS has a very interesting mix of incentives in its organization, which have been very effective in creating both short- and long-term opportunities for its employees and, seemingly, in generating enthusiasm and improved retention. In fact, HCSS was the recipient of the NCEO's Innovation Award at the annual NCEO/Beyster Institute annual conference in 2008. The incentives the company offers include the following:

- An annual profit-sharing plan tied to the organization's overall profit performance

- An ESOP

- Stock appreciation rights (SARs)

HCSS has had some interesting challenges along the Ownership Thinking path related to incentives and has approached

these challenges in a very thoughtful manner (as it does all things).
I asked Mike to provide me with his thoughts in this area so that I
could include them here, and this is what he sent me:

> In our ESOP, we ended up with the situation where we
> had "haves" and "have nots." There are 20 "haves" enjoying
> the success of the company and 90 "have nots" who were
> largely driving growth but not receiving the benefits of that.
> We are an S-Corp and not 100% ESOP, so the S-Corp dis-
> tributions result in making the ESOP cash accounts of the
> "haves" much larger than everyone else's—so they continue
> to get all of the stock that comes available. Therefore, we
> introduced SARs to new employees that automatically vest
> and cash out in 4 years. The intent is to give new employees
> an incentive to build the company and be concerned about
> the stock value while their ESOP account is still very small.
> Because of the recession, the stock value hasn't increased
> enough to make this exciting at this time. More effective
> long term is the 10% diversification described below.
>
> In an attempt to move stock from the "haves" to the
> "have nots," we started a 10% diversification program where
> any 100% vested ESOP employee can roll up to 10% of their
> ESOP stock each year to an IRA (or take cash with the 10%
> penalty). For the first two years of this program, all of the
> "haves" have diversified, thus freeing up more stock for the
> rest of the employees. We have decided to cap our ESOP
> at 30% because we feel that at that rate we can handle any
> repurchase obligation for employees who retire or leave
> the company, hence the need to free up stock from existing

ESOP shareholders. In addition, it further diversifies our ESOP shareholder base thus reducing even further the possibility that we would need a lot of cash to pay a few people who left at the same time. The problem with counting on this is the possibility that some employees will hang on to their stock and not share with the other employees, and I'm afraid there is nothing we can do about it. If many of your "haves" are greedy, you defeat the purpose of an ESOP as a tool to involve all of the employees, and it simply becomes an exit strategy for an owner and a way for a few more people to become owners.

The key thing I want to pass along about an ESOP is that there are quite a few surprises when setting one up, and you shouldn't take it lightly. I knew a lot about ESOPs when we established ours, but apparently not enough. My opinion now is that you should be very generous with profit sharing to encourage employees to build up equity for the owner/ owners, and be very cautious with sharing stock. As you know, we give 60% profit sharing after the threshold which gives employees a huge incentive to exceed the threshold. I have the impression that this is much more effective at creating an interest in the business than equity and has none of the downsides. In addition, employees working to drive up the profit sharing will ultimately be a good deal for the owner, so it encourages owners to generously share profits.

Having said all of this, I am not disappointed that we have an ESOP—it was just way more difficult than I had anticipated. One good benefit was that I was able to partially cash out with a favorable tax treatment. We also now have

191

a mini stock market to trade our stock and an evaluation every year to set a stock value which we use for all trades. We can give private company stock as management incentives, and, if they ever want to cash out, the company either repurchases at the ESOP rate or the ESOP can purchase it. While no one outside of the ESOP is obligated to sell at ESOP rates, nevertheless the history of using ESOP rates sets a precedent that has worked so far. We therefore have far more flexibility with stock than most private companies [do]. In addition there are a substantial number of employees with large ESOP accounts who are dedicated to making the company succeed.

Final Thoughts on ESOPs

The examples above may give you some pause when it comes to considering an ESOP. I do think it's important to take them to heart and to do your homework before going down the ESOP road. Having said that, it is statistically borne out that ESOPs are generally successful no matter how you measure them, but it should be clear based on the information in this chapter that it is very important to focus on building an ownership culture in addition to the technical aspects of the ESOP.

┌─────────────────────────┐
│ **KEY CONCEPTS** │
└─────────────────────────┘

- A company need not be an ESOP to practice Ownership Thinking, but ESOP companies must create an Ownership Thinking culture if they are to benefit from the plan.

- ESOP companies that do not do the cultural work will generally underperform against their non-ESOP competitors.

- An ESOP is fundamentally a retirement plan tied to the value of the company's equity.

- There are a variety of tax and other financial benefits to having an ESOP.

- Employees typically do not contribute to their ESOPs; rather, contributions are funded by the company as a benefit.

- Merely creating an ESOP will not create an Ownership Thinking culture.

- There are many complexities that must be addressed when considering an ESOP. Do your homework and get help (the NCEO is a good resource).

CHAPTER SEVEN

Ownership Thinking for the Long Term

C ompanies are pretty good at starting things, but not very good at following through with them. I will be discussing several suggestions in this final chapter that will help you to successfully implement and, more important, sustain Ownership Thinking in your organization. Let's start with the most important, which is involving the stakeholders in its implementation.

One of the most common reasons that initiatives fail (or never realize their full potential) is that the stakeholders are not involved in the implementation and follow-through of the initiatives. Business owners or leaders will read a book, hear of a successful strategy from a friend, hear a speaker, or be exposed to something in a group they belong to and become enthused (and perhaps hooked). So they run back to their respective organizations and push the initiative down on all of their employees, without carefully explaining the initiative and its purpose, much less involving them in the implementation itself. Now, I don't know about you, but I know what I do if people try to push an idea down on me: I push back. Why? Because it's not my idea, it's theirs. Without a strong understanding of the initiative, its value, *or its effect on me*, I will be less likely to support it. And without involvement, I will be unlikely to become an advocate. People become advocates of what they understand, appreciate, and take ownership of.

What I've outlined is the reason for the "flavor-of-the-month" syndrome that we see so often and hear about all the time.

In the above scenario, the owners or business leaders have taken the entire onus of the initiative's success on their own shoulders and without the support of those who will be affected. This will limit the potential success of the initiative and, since employees do not understand the value of the initiative or its potential positive or negative effect on them, they will most likely look for ways to sabotage it. As a business owner or leader, you have many things on your mind every day, so the resistance will typically win out and the initiative will go away. Do this often enough and you have taught all of your employees that they can outwait you and that they do not need to take your ideas very seriously.

One of the most effective ways to avoid having Ownership Thinking become the latest flavor-of-the-month, then, is to involve your employees in its implementation and make them responsible for its ongoing success. We will address the ongoing success of Ownership Thinking later in the chapter. Here are some suggestions for employee involvement in its implementation:

1. Discuss the initiative with your senior leadership team members first. Explain what it is about, what it is meant to achieve, how it will be implemented, what they might expect relative to their role in it, how it may change the dynamics between management and employees, and why you think it is important to them and to the organization (another option would be to have them attend an Ownership Thinking event, such as the annual conference). It's a good idea to have someone of influence on the team already in your camp before this discussion, so I

suggest you identify that person and ensure that he or she is on board before assembling the whole leadership team. At the meeting, be prepared to field questions and have some debate. You may want to show the team the video from the home page of the Ownership Thinking Web site. *Important point:* Ownership Thinking implies high involvement, information sharing, and transparency, *but does not imply consensus management or democracy*. If you are the business owner and/or CEO, and if you believe that Ownership Thinking is the right thing for your organization and for (most of) its members, then ultimately the decision to go forward should be yours.

2. Have a WGO (What's Going On) meeting with all employees (or several meetings if the company is large and/or geographically dispersed) to explain Ownership Thinking and to field questions. Explain what employees can expect and how they will be involved.

3. Survey your employees, as noted in Chapter 4. Let them know that, even though they will not be present at the Key Indicator workshop (which is typically attended by management only), the information they provide in the surveys will play a part in that discussion and in determining the organization's Key Performance Indicators (KPIs) and direction.

4. Create a financial trend analysis.

5. Involve all your management team members in the Key Indicator workshop, as outlined in Chapter 4. Again, their involvement not only will help to ensure that the proper KPIs and Rapid Improvement Plans (RIPs) are identified, but will create ownership of the process and its outcomes, thus creating advocacy and an ability to effectively communicate these outcomes to employees.

6. Also, involve your management team in the design of the incentive plan. Remember that Ownership Thinking does not connote consensus management, though. The final "blessing" of the plan will likely fall on the shoulders of the owner, CEO, and/or board. Explain this to your management team members during any discussions you may have about the plan so that they don't have unrealistic expectations.

7. Once the foundation of the initiative is built (KPIs identified, scoreboard designed, incentive plan formalized, first few RIPs drafted, and so on), have an official Ownership Thinking kick-off meeting with all employees. Introduce the various components of the initiative as noted above and have time for Q&A. Make it fun and memorable. It is, generally, a good rule of thumb that this meeting and meetings like it are not facilitated by the owner or CEO but rather by other people in the organization who may or may not be in management roles and who are respected at all levels.

The Adult Contract

In Chapter 1, we examined the issue of entitlement and the effect of entitlement on organizations and organization members. Then we discussed "the good news" and introduced the concept of earning cultures as opposed to cultures of entitlement. My experience tells me that people are far happier *and* productive in an earning environment, in large part because their lives are more purposeful. However, it is not easy to move from an entitlement culture to a culture of earning, and it is likely to create some fear. Let's face it: any change is a little scary, but particularly when accountability is attached to it.

I think it's important to address the issue of fear as it relates to making this change. Fear is often associated with anxiety, and I think, in this case, it's important to differentiate between the two of them. Organizations that are truly fear driven are typically autocratic, top-down cultures where employees are kept in the dark and not engaged. This is sometimes called "mushroom management," for which I've provided a definition from Wikipedia:

> *Mushroom management* is an allusion to a company's staff being treated like mushrooms: kept in the dark, covered with dung, and, when grown big enough, canned (fired). The connotation is that the management is making decisions without consulting the staff affected by those decisions, and possibly not even informing the staff until well after such decisions are made.

I suppose you could say that people are anxious in this environment; but, of course, that is a negative energy, which I would call fear. These are typically unproductive environments and are no fun. Furthermore, these environments may perform well in the short term, as measured by financial results, but they are not sustainable.

I need to point out, however, that there is actually a fair amount of anxiety in cultures of earning, although it is a different kind of energy. It is an entrepreneurial energy, an energy around winning. I am pointing this out because if you proceed down the path to Ownership Thinking, you will create an environment of high visibility and high accountability, and you will do this in fairly short order. This energy is critical to achieving a high performing and purposeful work environment. If, historically, there has been a fairly low level of visibility and accountability in your organization, and if you have even somewhat of an entitlement culture, then your employees will become anxious, and initially this will be felt as fear. As I said before, anything new is a bit scary, particularly when accountability is attached to it. One of the ways this fear manifests itself is through finger-pointing and blame. This is perfectly normal, but it is important to be prepared for it. Here is what you *do not want to do*. Do not freak out and go running back to entitlement. If you allow this to happen, then you will have allowed this normal resistance to accountability to prevent positive and constructive change in your organization. Also, you will have reinforced the entitlement culture that is holding everyone back from greater achievement and purpose, which, of course, means that you are not doing anyone any favors. You've got to tough it out.

With this in mind, I suggest that you implement something we call "The Adult Contract" in your organization in conjunction with Ownership Thinking (see Figure 7.1). This does not need to be a written document, and no one needs to sign anything. It is simply an agreement as to how people ought to treat one another in this new environment of visibility and accountability. If I were to state The Adult Contract, it would be something like this: "We agree that we are all adults here. We are probably all here for the same reasons; to work in a company that provides competitive financial remuneration, a fun and challenging environment, and security *for those who earn it*. Toward that end, we will act like adults, and there are certain things that adults do and certain things that they do not do."

The Adult Contract

OWNERSHIP THINKING

"We agree that we are all adults here"
We would all like the same things from our work:
- An enjoyable and rewarding environment
- A place to learn and grow
- Financial opportunities

Adults Don't:	Adults Do:
○ Shoot each other	○ Respect one another
○ Hide problems	○ Help one another
○ Argue with reality	○ Protect their home and family

FIGURE 7.1

For example, adults do not shoot each other (figuratively, of course). The reasons for this are quite obvious. If employees are honest and caring enough to own up to mistakes they've made, and they get shot for that, it's pretty clear what they will do the next time they make mistakes (they'll hide them, of course). If they try out ideas and they don't work and they get shot for that, it's pretty clear what they will do with their next ideas (they'll keep them to themselves). Adults also don't hide problems. They recognize that if a problem remains hidden, it won't be addressed much less rectified, and it will probably get worse. Finally, adults don't argue with reality. Guess what—no amount of argument will change reality. Adults simply address reality and deal with it, even if that means making painful decisions in the short term to ensure future stability and success.

Let me elaborate on that last point: *Adults don't argue with reality*. As of this writing, our country is on the tail end (we hope, at least) of a significant downturn in the economy, which companies have been dealing with for a few years. There is an interesting area of study known as *learned helplessness*, which is a condition of a human being or an animal in which it has learned to behave helplessly, even when the opportunity is restored for it to help itself by avoiding an unpleasant or harmful circumstance to which it has been subjected. In the current economy, you may begin hearing excuses for poor performance, which employees may express by blaming the economy, market conditions, the competition, and so on. This is an example of learned helplessness in the workplace.

Yes, economic conditions may be rough at times. However, regardless of the economic conditions (or any other circumstances, for that matter), some companies will win, and some companies will lose. The winning companies (and people) will be those that accept reality for what it is and make the decisions and take the actions that will get them through successfully. And as adults, they know that the short-term pain will be rewarded in the long run. At the end of the downturn (and it will end), they will have their "A team" in place (having made some tough personnel decisions), they will have best practices in place (such as Ownership Thinking), and they will have less competition, because some companies decided to argue with reality.

There are other things adults do, as well. They respect one another. They help one another. They take responsibility (and they don't pass blame). They remain calm in the face of adversity or failure (and they simply try again). Finally, they protect their homes and their families. On this last point, I mean that in a business environment we protect our company and our coworkers. For example, if a company decides to share more financial information with its employees, the employees must agree not to share that information outside of the organization. Would it hurt the company if they did? Probably not (see Chapter 3), but why take that chance?

I encourage you to talk openly about these things when you go down the Ownership Thinking path. Let employees know that it is new for everyone, including you, and that everyone will be taking this journey together. Reinforce the fact that nobody is perfect at anything when they are learning for the first time; we get better by practicing (I'm a big fan of the Nike catchphrase, "Just Do It"). Talk them through The Adult Contract, and tell them to be watching for nonadult behavior, starting with themselves.

I had a client some time ago who did something rather clever. The company leaders recognized that historically they had something of a fear-driven environment and that people were familiar with "getting shot." To introduce The Adult Contract, everyone in the company received a "Get Out of Jail Free" card. The idea was that if any employees made a mistake or tried out something that didn't work, they had this card to let them off the hook. Of course it was symbolic, but it made a great point and did so in a lighthearted manner.

Creating an Ownership Thinking Steering Committee

When working with clients, we generally help them form an Ownership Thinking Steering Committee (OTSC) to ensure that the initiative survives and thrives. There are many definitions of steering committees out there, but I'll offer one that is an amalgam of a few that I've seen:

> A steering committee is a group of stakeholders who are responsible for providing guidance on overall strategic direction. They help to spread the strategic input and buy in to a larger portion of the organization. The steering committee is usually made up of organizational peers and is the combination of direct customers and indirect stakeholders.

I typically suggest that the OTSC have no more than five to eight members (less in a very small organization and perhaps a few more in a large one—particularly if there are multiple locations or business units). Two or three of the members (no more) should be from the management team and the remaining members from nonmanagement (though perhaps supervisory) roles that represent different functions and/or geographic areas of the organization. Members should want to be on the committee. They should be high energy, respected members of the organization who will be supportive of the Ownership Thinking philosophy and effort. When getting started with Ownership Thinking, the management team should identify the first OTSC (the committee can determine how future members will be identified). These people should then be asked if they would like to participate rather than be required to do so. Members should be rotated in and out of the committee (perhaps every six months to a year) in order to keep it fresh and allow others to participate. The committee can decide how this will be done.

I like the idea of the OTSC having its own mission statement. In my language, a mission statement is about defining why something exists. Here is one of my favorite mission statements from one of our client OTSCs:

> The Ownership Thinking Steering Committee is the *corporate conscience* for Ownership Thinking, ensuring that we have full engagement through effective *communication* and the use of Ownership Thinking tools such as *Rapid Improvement Plans, scoreboards, and incentive plans.*

The OTSC detailed its objectives as follows:

1. Corporate Conscience

   a. Cheerlead.

   b. Keep it honest (ensure that the process is being followed).

   c. Have fun and instigate fun.

   d. Ask questions to ensure involvement and clarity among employees.

2. Communication

   a. Huddle information is regularly communicated at the department and organization levels.

   b. Organize employee WGO meetings (typically monthly or quarterly).

   • Financial update and incentive status (hand out checks when earned)

   • Rapid Improvement Plan updates

   • Financial acumen training (one topic at each meeting)

   • Significant events in the organization and in the lives of organization members

   • Fun!

    c. Promote departmental meetings.

    d. Encourage engagement and involvement.

    e. Create and maintain a monthly communiqué.

3. RIPs

    a. Identify a pool of RIP opportunities based on submissions.

    b. Select RIPs and the timing of their implementation (communicate to leadership team).

    c. Identify people and/or departments who should be involved in the design, and go through design exercise.

    d. Ensure that at least one RIP is underway at any given time (two or three is fine, as long as it is not overwhelming).

(*Note:* I believe that the most important function of the OTSC is to ensure that RIPs are being developed, implemented, communicated, and celebrated.)

Being on a steering committee can be a bit tricky, so you will need to be cautious. The steering committee and its members do not want to be seen as the Enforcers of Ownership Thinking. The Cops. I have seen this happen, and it is not pretty. An OTSC that is perceived this way will ultimately be disrespected by employees, who will not participate in, and perhaps even sabotage, the initiative. In addition, Enforcers will probably not be supported by leadership. So, committee members find themselves between a rock and a hard place, and *they* become miserable as well. A good steering committee needs to become adept at *influencing without authority*. This has far more to do with educating, informing, and participating than it does with enforcing. This, by the way, is what a good consultant does: influence without authority. The best book I have ever read on this subject, hands down, is *Flawless Consulting,* by Peter Block. I recommend it to anyone in a position of having to create change without having the authority to dictate change. In fact, it would be helpful for anyone in a leadership role (who does have authority) to read this book.

The Role of the CEO

I have noted many times in this book that the onus of the success of Ownership Thinking should not fall on the shoulders of the owner and / or CEO. What, then, is the role of the CEO, and what might he or she do to ensure the success of Ownership Thinking? I believe the most important role of the CEO is (1) to be committed to the implementation of Ownership Thinking, which means allowing for the resources necessary to ensure its success, and (2) to communicate this commitment whenever and wherever possible. Any new initiative, much less one as comprehensive as Ownership Thinking, will be met with some resistance. When this occurs, the CEO must be prepared to point out that a solution to any obstacle must be found and that the solution will not be to abandon the Ownership Thinking initiative. The CEO should offer confidence that the brainpower to overcome any implementation problems is most likely in the organization, but if not, then there are resources outside of the organization that can be tapped, such as members of the Ownership Thinking staff. It should be quite clear that abandonment is not an option.

Here are three of the most common forms of resistance that I have heard over the years and suggestions on how to address them:

- "I don't have time for all this; I have my job to do. You want me to do my job, don't you?" Whenever I hear this form of resistance, I answer it in exactly the same way and that is, "This *is* your job." Ownership Thinking is simply an effective mechanism to accomplish the objectives and strategies in an organization in a high-involvement and enlightened fashion. Like anything else, however, it does take practice. Encourage employees to keep trying and to respect the fact that they (and their coworkers) are learning and are likely to make mistakes and feel awkward for a while.

- "Our technology (or accounting system) is not sophisticated enough to support this." The truth is, Ownership Thinking does not require particularly sophisticated technologies or accounting systems. Most things can be measured where they happen and with fairly unsophisticated mechanisms. I've seen some simplistic yet fantastically effective reporting mechanisms, such as a grease board on a shop floor or a tally sheet in an office. When challenged with identifying a method of tracking and reporting a KPI, most employees will rise to the occasion and come up with something quite creative and effective.

- The last of the three, and perhaps the most irritating (to me, at any rate), typically comes from people in management roles. It goes something like this: "This all sounds great, but, of course, it won't work in the 'real world.'" I say this is irritating to hear because it infers that I live somewhere else. This comment is meant to make the change go away by making it sound impractical or even silly. Ownership Thinking is immensely practical. Companies practicing it are financially and culturally successful, often extraordinarily so. But it is a different approach to business, and it requires some effort and perseverance. It is worth it.

These challenges are quite common, and should be addressed head on.

Another way the CEO can ensure that Ownership Thinking is taking hold (without spearheading it) is to ask lots of questions while roaming about the organization. You've probably heard the term *Management by Walking Around* (*MBWA*), which was made popular by Tom Peters in the 1980s. This term means that a CEO cannot really know what's happening in the organization without having personal interaction with employees throughout the organization and that this is best done in a somewhat informal fashion. Here are some of the suggestions regarding this method of management:

- Wander about as often as you can, but recurrently and preferably daily.

- Share and invite good news.

- Watch and listen without judgment.

- Invite ideas and opinions to improve operations, products, services, and so on.

- Be responsive to problems and concerns.

- Look out for staff doing something right, and give them public recognition.

- Give people on-the-spot help.

- Use the opportunity to transmit the organization's values.

I would add to that list: ask questions about the Ownership Thinking initiative. The underlying idea here is that you really don't know if people understand something until they explain it to you. I've learned this firsthand over the years, but particularly in my role as president of Mrs. Fields in Mexico. In that role, I would ask someone if he or she understood such-and-such, and the response was inevitably "yes," or "of course." Did I know whether that person really understood it? Of course not. People generally respond this way because they don't want to appear ignorant, don't want additional work, or don't want to get their supervisors in trouble. Here are some examples of questions for MBWA in an Ownership Thinking culture:

- Tell me about the Rapid Improvement Plan that's currently underway. What's your role in that? How are we doing against the goal? I've forgotten what the celebration is for that one—do you know?

- Can you explain your incentive plan? How are we doing this quarter against the plan, and how does it look for an incentive this quarter?

- What are the Key Indicators that your department is focused on? How are you doing with them?

One of the most effective MBWA leaders I've seen who uses this method is Zimmerman Boulos. I've seen him go so far as to ask an employee at a WGO meeting to come up front and show everyone on the chalkboard what a profit and loss statement (key areas such as revenue, cost of goods, overhead, and profit) looks like in a typical company in the industry and how the company compares. As I write this chapter I am on a plane to Florida, where (among other engagements) I will be spending some time at Zimmerman's company to do a refresher. The company, OE&S, was one of my early clients, so it has been some time since I've been there. The survey results and financial analysis I did prior to this visit absolutely blew me away. Prior to implementing Ownership Thinking, this company had experienced some pretty tough times. It had a dramatic turnaround in the first year after implementing the plan, and I was happy to see that it has sustained this upward swing. Its financials and survey results clearly exhibit a best-in-class company (and a 70 percent increase in revenue since

213

it implemented the plan), the performance of which far exceeds industry standards.

To end this section on the CEO's role, here is a passage from Peter Block's book, *Flawless Consulting*:

> If you look at the great leaders through history, you see a consciousness of their own limitations that was essential to their greatness. From Confucius, Buddha, and Christ, to Lincoln, Gandhi, and Martin Luther King—all touched lives because of their presence more than their position. They became archetypes for the right use of power, and one source of their power was their own humility.
>
> Power used to distance ourselves from our prescriptions is power abused. And don't think that leaders are alone in thinking others should be the ones to change. The love of patriarchy is as strong in employees as in management. Employees create bosses. If we create high-control bosses, we consider ourselves entitled, and entitlement means that we are not the problem: Something is due us, and we owe nothing. We hold to the safety of our dependency, just as the boss does, and each of us thinks the other needs to be fixed.

Mission-Driven and Not-For-Profit Organizations

When working with not-for-profit organizations, I have found that my approach has to be different than with for-profit companies because the not-for-profits are quite often more mission driven than money driven (certainly at the employee level). The same applies when working with for-profit companies that are particularly mission driven. Examples of for-profit, mission-driven companies I've worked with include an elder care company, a healthy dog and cat food retail chain, and a company that provides nursing support to Medicare patients.

I'll never forget the first time I implemented Ownership Thinking in an organization like this. It was a company in the health-care industry, and when I began talking about the importance of earnings performance, I thought the employees were going to fall out of their chairs. The reaction was basically "we're not here to make money; we're here to save lives!" After this experience, I did some research on the issue and came across a story about a Catholic nun who managed several very successful hospitals—and with somewhat of an iron glove, it seemed. Her mantra was: "No margin, no mission!" In other words, of course we are here to save lives (our mission). However, if we want to deliver a big mission and save a lot of lives, then it takes money to do that. So the creation of earnings (or profit) is more about the ability to deliver a bigger mission than satisfying shareholders or funding an incentive plan. Since then, I have emphasized this thinking in these types of cultures, and with very good results.

Multilocation Organizations

I recently sat in on a huddle with Mud Bay, a healthy dog and cat food retail chain with, at the time of this writing, over 20 locations

215

throughout the Seattle area. (Keep your eyes open for this chain wherever you live—this is a beautiful concept very well executed, and I am quite sure it will be expanding quickly.) While I was there, the employees were still fairly new to Ownership Thinking, having implemented with us approximately one year prior to this visit. I was very impressed with their process, the serious yet celebratory nature of it, the knowledge of the participants, and the obvious effect they had on results.(This was particularly rewarding to see because only one year earlier the store managers were clearly not very sophisticated from a numbers standpoint).

As with most of our clients who have multiple locations (or business units in different regions), the chain used a Web-based tool to facilitate reporting and sharing KPIs. Aside from myself and one of my Super Group members (explained later), there were six people in the room at the corporate office for this meeting: the two owners, the two regional managers (we'll call them regions one and two), the person in charge of purchasing and internal distribution, the marketing director, and someone from finance. The scoreboard was up on a flat-panel monitor in front of the room, and the representative from finance was at the keyboard, ready to input information. The store managers from region one were on a conference line, and all were able to view the scoreboard from their respective locations. Each store had a tab on the scoreboard, and the respective store managers went through their numbers while the finance person populated the scoreboard, in real time, as they did so. Highlights were briefly celebrated, and opportunities for improvement were briefly addressed (and it was clear that actions on those opportunities for improvement would be taken after the meeting). When region one finished, these managers got off the line, and the same process was repeated for region two. Upon completion of region two, the region one managers rejoined the call, and companywide results (which were automatically populated on a roll-up tab) were briefly reviewed. This entire process took roughly one hour, and upon its conclusion, the leadership from throughout the company knew exactly where the company was headed for that month (and year to date), what strategies were particularly successful (so that others could learn from them), and what opportunities needed to be addressed before the next huddle. This information could then be passed on to team members in the stores and corporate office.

What I just described is a great example of an efficient and effective Ownership Thinking process in a multilocation company (kudos to Mud Bay!). Based on this example and my experience in other multilocation companies, here are some tips:

- The location scoreboards should be fairly simple and straightforward in these companies, particularly if there are more than three or four and/or if the location-level managers have not had a great deal of profit and loss knowledge or accountability prior to practicing Ownership Thinking.

- Find a Web-based tool that works best for you. There are several to choose from, and many are available at no cost. At Ownership Thinking, where we also have people from different locations participating in our huddles, we are using Google Docs. This is a free tool that enables us to view our scoreboard in real time. In addition—and very cool, I might add—control of the spreadsheet does not have to be passed from one participant to another; anyone can work on it at any time during the call.

- As with any huddle, it is important that participants understand the critical importance of their presence. If one person is not present, it throws a wrench into the whole exercise and then has an effect on the roll-up accuracy. If someone cannot be present, then he or she must have someone from the operation to stand in.

- It's easy to lose track of time in a huddle of this complexity. Avoid getting into too much detail on any one location and ensure that there is a mechanism for following up where necessary (in the case of Mud Bay, the regional managers would do the follow-up after the meeting). Have an agenda and stick to it.

Dealing with Poor Performing Individuals, Departments, or Business Units

Obviously, different people have different levels of experience, education, and confidence and will become adept at practicing Ownership Thinking based on these unique characteristics and backgrounds. It is important to allow for a few months to pass before making a determination as to anyone's ability to succeed in this new environment of visibility and accountability. Those people who may be struggling should be offered the information and training they need to come up to speed. Although most of these employees will indeed improve after three or four months of comparing actuals to budgets and forecasts, you will likely experience one or more of the following:

- A few people may opt out (leave the organization). Quite often these will be your poorest performers and perhaps those employees who were able to survive in the past because they had become very adept at hiding (often in "busyness"). They can no longer do this, of course, and their true performance becomes quite clear. This is obviously uncomfortable for them, and they will often choose to leave the organization of their own accord (in fact, their peers may help them with this decision). This, in my opinion, is a good thing.

- In some cases, it might become clear that individuals who are engaged and working hard to be successful still do not have the right skill sets to do so in their respective roles. In these cases (assuming they have been given training and all the information about their job they need), it may be possible to find them different roles where they can be successful.

- Finally, there may be a few employees who clearly cannot perform effectively in their roles and do not exhibit qualities that make them candidates for different roles (or, perhaps, no other roles are available), yet refuse to leave the organization. My experience has been that these employees might actively try to sabotage the initiative by challenging its integrity or reliability. In any case, they probably need to be let go. As I noted earlier, it is profoundly unfair to everyone else in the organization to allow these individuals to damage everyone else's opportunities. Furthermore, this behavior damages the credibility of leadership (and of Ownership Thinking) if nothing is done. Tim Keran, owner of Western Graphics and a member of our Super Group, says it very nicely: "You can't quit and stay."

Just as you might encounter individuals who are having trouble performing their roles, you might find that one of your departments or business units is underperforming. If this is the case, you must make a determination as to why and then decide what needs to be done. If poor performance is due to the leadership in that area, then leadership must be improved, moved, or replaced. If the problem has to do with poor systems or strategy, then these must be addressed. The underlying theme here is (from The Adult Contract) that we don't argue with reality. Once we begin to ignore reality by allowing poor performance to go unaddressed, or by hiding it or minimizing it, then the integrity of Ownership Thinking is diminished. This is particularly important because everyone's incentive (and retirement, in the case of an Employee Stock Ownership Plan) is tied to the overall performance of the company.

Tapping Into the Ownership Thinking Community

Seeing Ownership Thinking touch and improve as many businesses and lives as possible (and to eradicate entitlement) is my mission in life, and the same could be said of everyone here in my organization. We have implemented this way of doing business in well over 1,000 companies, and our implementation process is very thorough and efficient. It is not nearly as time-consuming as one might think, either, generally taking no more than two to five days of on-site work, depending on the size of the organization. You need to know that initiatives have a tendency to lose steam over time (even one as powerful as Ownership Thinking), and the Ownership Thinking staff is available for any support needs you may have. In addition, we have also worked over the years to create a "community" of Ownership Thinking companies that support and help one another on their respective journeys, and we have developed the following tools to help them do this:

- **The Ownership Thinking Club (OTC).** The OTC is a membership area of our Web site that enables practitioners of Ownership Thinking to continue learning and growing. Members can participate in Webinars that are held every other month and that focus on various areas of Ownership Thinking and best practices in general. Over the past two years, topics have included RIPs, financial acumen training, key indicators and forecasting, accountability in health insurance plans, broad-based equity design, talent hiring and retaining, entitlement eradication, and others. These Webinars (as well as our "Tips" messages) are archived in the members' area so that they can be accessed at any time. There is also a dialogue page in the membership area that allows members to bring up issues and talk with other practitioners to find solutions and share ideas (similar to LinkedIn). Members also receive discounts on all Ownership Thinking events and products. For information about the OTC (and for other resources noted below), visit our Web site at www.ownershipthinking.com.

- **The Ownership Thinking Annual Conference.** Ownership Thinking hosted its first conference in the fall of 2007. This is now an annual two-day event held near Denver, Colorado, and is typically in late September or early October. Each year brings a new theme, and there are between 15 and 20 expert resource speakers at each conference, many of whom are business leaders and practitioners of Ownership Thinking. We have also had some outstanding keynote speakers over the years, including Judith Bardwick and Kim Jordan (CEO of New Belgium). What really sets this conference apart, however, is the exciting nature of its attendees: enlightened businesspeople who share the great qualities outlined in this book and who love to share and learn from one another. The conference is structured in such a way as to allow attendees to do this freely.

- **The Ownership Thinking "Tips and News."** This is a bimonthly message that goes out to all of our friends. It includes a variety of helpful information, including:

  - Useful tips from companies practicing Ownership Thinking, including things that have worked for them as well as things that have not worked so well. We encourage people to submit their experiences to us, since the idea is to learn from one another's successes and failures.

  - Tips from my experience and the experience of Ownership Thinking consultants.

  - Resources for support in a variety of areas, such as health care, exit planning, leadership development, valuations, internal communications, and budgeting.

  - Relevant and important books recommended by the Ownership Thinking staff (we are prolific readers here).

  - Quotes that are uplifting and/or thought provoking and that can be used in various business (and personal) settings.

  - Events that support the Ownership Thinking mission. These include ours, of course, but also events held by other organizations and associations.

- Log on to our Web site, and provide us with the information requested in the drop-down box on the home page (which is included in the bimonthly e-mailing).

■ **The Ownership Thinking Super Group.** Over the years, we have been blessed to work with some exceptional leaders, and we wanted to create a forum so these people can share their experiences and knowledge toward creating truly best-in-class companies. The Super Group was founded in early 2010 for this purpose, and it is an invitation-only group of CEOs and business leaders, all practitioners of Ownership Thinking, which meets three times per year. Two of these meetings are hosted by a member company (in its city), and the third takes place in Colorado prior to the annual conference. As opposed to many executive groups that focus primarily on issues or problems of members, the Super Group focuses on best practices and learning. Members bring a best practice to each meeting (something they do exceptionally well in their organizations) and share it with other members. In addition, members (I am one) read a book between each meeting and have a discussion around it. We encourage the CEOs to bring direct reports to each meeting so that they can develop ideas together afterwards, increasing the likelihood of something actually happening in their organizations based on what they've learned together. As the Super Group evolves and grows, we will start new chapters and likely create ways that these chapters can "cross-pollinate." Ultimately, I see these groups being the catalyst for the development and sharing of some truly exceptional business practices, as well as providing fodder for articles, books, and conference sessions.

The Importance of Moving to Mexico

Whenever I complete a session with a leadership team or group of employees, I like to close with the following little story, some of which I presented in the Introduction.

"In 1992, I was offered the job of president for Mrs. Fields Cookies in Mexico. The company was struggling, so it was a turnaround situation. After much internal debate and many conversations with family, friends, and business associates, I decided that, though obviously a significant challenge, it was an opportunity that I could not pass up. I packed all of the belongings I could fit into my Nissan Altima, and I moved to Mexico City.

"This was by far the most terrifying thing I had ever done. I didn't speak Spanish. I knew very few people, and I had no close friends in Mexico. I didn't understand the culture. And I was taking the reins of a company that was struggling. What was I thinking?

"My point here is that *I had moved to Mexico City*. I *had* to learn the language. I *had* to make friends and get involved in the business community. I *had* to get familiar with the culture. I *had* to get my arms around the company and the issues it was facing. I had no choice.

"Here is the thought I want to leave with you: I want you all to move to Mexico!"

I've told you this story because I want to emphasize the importance of committing to a process if you hope for success. All it takes for success are two things: (1) A great tool (Ownership Thinking is a phenomenal tool), and (2) the commitment to execute. My client companies that have committed to implementing Ownership Thinking according to our process have shown significant cultural and financial improvements in a matter of a few months and have changed their cultures entirely in a year or so. It's not easy, but the rewards are truly remarkable.

KEY CONCEPTS

■ Companies are good at starting things, but not very good at following through. In order to avoid creating another "flavor of the month" program, you need to do the following:

  • Involve your employees in the Ownership Thinking implementation process from start to finish.

  • Practice The Adult Contract.

  • The CEO should support the Ownership Thinking effort without actually leading it.

  • Ask questions of employees to ensure that they are engaged and informed.

  • Create an Ownership Thinking Steering Committee.

■ If you have a mission-driven company, make sure it focuses on the fact that in order to deliver a big mission, the company must make money (no margin, no mission).

■ Multilocation companies can effectively practice Ownership Thinking with a few additional communication tools.

■ Tap into the available resources to help you "stay the course" with Ownership Thinking.

■ It takes two things to create success: a great tool and the commitment to use it.

CLOSING THOUGHTS

In the Introduction, I suggested that this would not be your typical business book, that Ownership Thinking would require a significant level of participation and accountability from both leadership and employees, and that everyone would have to step up and take responsibility for their own destinies. I also told you that there were spiritual, psychological, political, and human (emotional) elements to business and that I would do my best to address these without being too contentious. I hope that I have provided you with a good understanding of what Ownership Thinking is, what it means, and how to pursue it. And I hope (with all my heart) that I've done so in a manner that has allowed for people of all backgrounds and beliefs to consider Ownership Thinking not only as a viable way of doing business, but as a critically important pursuit—a mission even—toward ending entitlement and creating accountability, purposefulness, and profit.

FURTHER READING

Bardwick, Judith, *Danger in the Comfort Zone*, New York: AMACOM, 1995

Block, Peter, *Flawless Consulting, Second Edition,* San Francisco: Jossey-Bass Pfeiffer, 2000

Gatto, John Taylor, *Weapons of Mass Instruction*, Gabriola Island, BC, Canada: New Society Publishers, 2009

Maslow, *Maslow on Management*, New York: John Wiley & Sons, Inc., 1998

Pink, Daniel, *Drive*, New York: Riverhead Books (Penguin Group), 2009

Rand, Ayn, *Atlas Shrugged*, New York: Penguin Group, 1999

———, *Capitalism, The Unknown Ideal*, New York: New American Library, 1967

Sykes, Charles, *50 Rules Kids Won't Learn in School*, New York: St. Martin's Press, 2007

INDEX

Brad Hams is founder and president of Ownership Thinking, LLC, a consulting and training firm that since 1995 has helped over 1,000 companies to unleash their true potential through employee education, engagement, and incentive strategies. Prior to that, he was president of Mrs. Fields Cookies in Mexico and held executive positions in a Fortune 100 company. Brad is a lifelong student of business and finance, holds a master's degree in organization development and human resources, and has taught business at the graduate level. He is a board member of the National Center for Employee Ownership and has contributed to several of its publications. Brad speaks to roughly 60 audiences a year in the United States and abroad, and is one of the most sought after speakers for Vistage, the world's largest membership organization of CEOs.